"MY LIFE V

"Walking on Clouds"

"A True Love Story"

By Dale Weatherford

1

My Life with Debbie

ISBN-13: 978-1494390310
ISBN-10: 1494390310

My life story begins...

Around the middle of 1966, I was living in the city of Commerce, California on Lantio Street. My family and I moved into an upstairs apartment consisting of my mom and my sister Dianna. It was a three bedroom apartment, but very small rooms. I really liked the bedroom I had at the back of the house. The reasoning behind this was looking out of my bedroom window I could see the screen of the Gage Driven Theatre. The family that lived below us, Alice and James the mother and stepfather, they had a son, Lloyd, and three sisters, Sharon, Sandra and little Debbie. This one sister of Lloyd's, the middle one in particular named "Debbie", she was eight years old and I was eleven years old... (A little background on Debbie Ann Morgan, she was born on August 8, 1958 in the city of Bellflower California to Alice Adamson and Manual Morgan)

I started hanging out with Lloyd. We both like the Beatles a lot so we had a lot in common. His sisters on the other hand were a pain in the butt. Especially Debbie, she would always play with her Barbie's on my steps going up to my apartment. She really aggravated me, like she did not care if she was in the way or not, she was always in my way.

One day I remembered coming down the stairs and of course she was playing again. I proceeded down the stairs and I gave her Barbie dolls a swift kick off the steps. She said, *"Dale one of these days I'm going to make you pay for that the rest of your life."*

Little did I know she would later hold me to that statement. I remember Debbie would make up imaginary girls and one in particular she called "Tony." She would say Tony told me that she likes you and of course I would believe her so would Lloyd, and later she would laugh and confess that she just made Tony up to see our reactions.

After they moved away we lost contact. I remember we lived there for a while still after they moved. I remember watching the movie "*Rose Mary's Baby*" on the theatre screen. This came out in 1968. It wasn't until my mother ran into David Sinclair, he was Debbie's mother's cousin. At Alice's house, Debbie's mother, they hit it off and start hanging out together. We visited them on occasion for a few years on and off. Lloyd and I stayed friends but it was hard to visit due to the distance from commerce to South Whittier, which was about thirty miles. In the mean time I was hanging out with the wrong crowd.

I was always into some sort of trouble with the law. Nothing more than mischievous things like curfew violation, and a lot of being in the wrong place at the wrong time. I dropped out of school in the ninth grade, along with my best friend Robert Cummins who I met in the seventh grade at Bell Gardens Jr. High School, and that is also the same time I met Jack Waver. He was another close friend, but a bit more "conservative." Robert and I was nothing but an uncontrollable "loose cannons."

We tried to hitch hike to Hollywood, sunset and vine, at least twice a month; that is where everyone in the late sixties - 1968 and 1969 a lot of young kids hung out. I was heading on a downhill run pretty fast and could not see the light of day. Due to all my troubles I was placed on probation. My probation officer suggested that I join Job Corps. So I enlisted and was sent by Greyhound Bus to Roseburg Oregon.

I was told lies about the center; now think about this, back then these probation officers were paid $50 a head to convince youths to join Job Corps. The probation officers painted this plush picture of the girls' center right across the road from the boys' center. They also had bowling, movie theaters and all kinds of entertainment.

Well, once I made it to Roseburg Oregon I was met by a counselor, got on another bus and was driven up the mountain road about twenty miles to the center in Guild, Oregon .

The guys here, most of them were hard core youths. And the girls' center was across the road and about two hundred miles away. No bowling, no theaters, and nothing of what you could call "entertainment."

We were packed in a dorm with thirty other guys and there was no privacy. We all looked like we were in the army; we wore army uniforms and combat boots. We went to school every other week, went to work every other week, and we would build rest areas in the mountains. "Manual labor." I stayed focused on trying to stay out of trouble and

4

tried to finish school. Everyone in school worked at their own level, so you could accelerate at your on speed.

I was at the center for about eight months to a year. I cannot quite remember for sure how long it was, but I did make it to eleventh grade. One afternoon this guy knew I lived around the Los Angeles area and he wanted to go home. He asked if I would sneak out with him and go home. I thought for a bit and said *"I had enough of this. Yes I leave with you."* I asked *"How much money do you have?"* He said *"Nothing, but I have 9 packs of cigarettes and had twenty five cents."* So we left the center and we made our way back to California in about 3 days. What an adventure that was in its self.

Once I got back home my mom was upset that I left the center and of course I did not much care. My mom is dating David Sinclair now and they are very serious, even talking marriage. David is Debbie's mom's cousin, no blood line between the two of us or that would make odd situation. One day David and my mom wanted me to go over to see them and of course it had been a long time since I have seen Lloyd.

So we went over to Alice and James Leonard's house. He was a truck driver for Transport Carriage.

So once we got to their house I started hanging out with Lloyd. After a few visits I started noticing his sister Debbie was turning thirteen years old.

I was sixteen and this was the year 1972. Debbie and I started talking every now and then. And then I started looking forward to having a conversation with her. There was something in her smile and I felt a glow radiating whenever she came into the room. She had this attraction that started drawing me into her. We started hitting it off and we were connecting very well. We both were confused on how well we were in tune with each other. We could talk for a long period of time and not even notice time.

I was confused on my inner feelings for Debbie. Now I'm trying to hitch hike to Lloyd's house to hang out and pretend to see Lloyd, but wanting to be around Debbie. Her smile and those beautiful blue eyes captured my heart; I was so attracted to her personality I could not get enough. I noticed she was feeling the same as I was, but she hid it better than I could. After a while I think her mom was starting to get wise of what was going on between me and Debbie, especially when I would show up and Lloyd would not be home so I would sit and talk to Debbie. I remember one day Debbie said her mom told her she should not get too involved with me. Her mom asked what is going on and Debbie said nothing, we just talk.

But of course I still did not hide my wanting to visit with Debbie. I knew I needed to start looking for work and landed a job at Taco Bell in Bell Gardens, this was the very first Taco Bell to ever to Taco Bell to open, and this was the start of the famous chain.

By this time everyone in Debbie's family was" hip" to our feelings for each other, it was so obvious we were in love and it was hard to keep us apart. I remember late nights at her house we would sit and play a game called *"Kismet"* sometimes till 10:00 or 11:00 pm and her mom would say, *"Ok Debbie, I think it's time to go to bed you got school in the morning."* Debbie absolutely loved this game and we would play for hours; I enjoyed it so much because we were interacting with each other.

Sometime after work at Taco Bell, Debbie would talk her Dad into driving over and picking me up after work in Bell Gardens. Debbie and her Dad were very close, she had his heart, and he loved her very much and would do anything for her. So before I would leave work I would make up a bunch of food; taco, burrito, and Debbie's mom loved taco bell coffee. I made sure I had quite a few packed so she could make a few pots of coffee. Debbie's dad and mom were getting very comfortable with me, I felt they were getting use to me and growing to like me very much.

Debbie and I became a "pair." We would go and hang out with my brother and his girl Jennie. He had separated from his wife Dreama. He and Jeannie were living together.

I remember us going up to Big Bear during the weather and sliding in the snow on those round toboggans. We would make a train rapping our legs around each other and sliding down the side of the mountain. These were some great times and only the beginning. We would go with my brother and Jeannie to Magic Mountain, we hung out together a lot.

I spent every minute I could with Debbie and she did not seem to mind that at all, our love was so well timed in life. When I was not working I would wait until about noon and then I would start my journey hitching to Whittier, about 30 miles to her house, sometimes I would get there around 4:00pm or sometimes 7:00 pm depending on how good of rides I was able to catch. By this time Debbie's mom would let me spend the night; I would sleep on the couch in the living room or one of the back bedrooms.

We were getting along so well that I went out and bought her and engagement ring at this pawn shop in Bell Gardens across the street from Taco Bell. I was so proud of it! So the next time I was over her house I presented it to her. She slips it on her ring finger and it fit perfect!

After a few weeks I started noticing she was not wearing the "ring" and I ask what was going on and why are she was not wearing my ring. Debbie said, her mother did not like the ideal of me getting this for her. Of course this made me very upset, and told her I did not care what her mom said. Of course Debbie was doing this out of respect for her mom. I was too stubborn to listen to reasoning, and flew of the handle and told her, "If you cannot wear my ring then we should end this relationship." she called by bluff and said *"OK."*

This left me speechless; I remember walking up the street towards the corner with this empty feeling in my stomach. I proceed to hitch hike home, being very humble and confused of what I just did.

I got home that evening and the next day I called Debbie but one of her sisters answered the phone. I asked for Debbie and she said, *"Debbie does not want to talk to you."* and hung up.
I was feeling very, very sorry for what I did. I did not want to hurt her, and I was hurting so much inside I felt out of place.

This went on for about a week and I remember my mom and I driving down Florence Ave. in Downey and in front of us was Jim and Alice, and Debbie was in the back seat. I saw her look back at me from the back seat and my heart just fell apart. I needed her back at any expense.

Later that evening I went to work at Taco Bell and I was feeling so ashamed of myself. My friend Robert, who was working the late shift with me, we decided to buy some beer. So Robert called up our friend

Mike Bozik to come by and drop off a couple of six-packs. Well, we kept the beer in the deep freezer and started drinking and got very drunk, and of course our boss came by and we were fired on the spot.

I walked down the street to a pay phone and I called Debbie's house, and her dad answered. I said, *"Jim can I please talk to Debbie?"* and I could hear him call Debbie to the phone. She picked up the phone and said, *"Hello."* Before she could say anything I said, *"Debbie I'm so sorry, please forgive me. I understand your respect for you mom and I will never make you decide between me and your mom, again, I do not want you to wear my ring if your mom disapproves, just take me back."* Of course I was in tears and she forgave me, I was so happy. But now I'm jobless and I did confess how I lost my job.

Even though I was fired, I had my Debbie back, and that was all that mattered. We started fantasizing and talking about marriage. Of course Debbie is only fourteen years old and I'm seventeen years old. But the time we were apart really affected us and knew in our hearts that this could not happen again.

So we talked about me getting a good stable job, and I started thinking about my sister who lives in Texas and her husband Johnny is a roofer. I said to Debbie, *"What if I call my sister and see if I could get a job as a roofer. I could take some time off after a while and we could get married and move to Texas."* Debbie's eyes lit up and said that was a great ideal.

I went home and told my mom that I was going to call Donna and see if I could go stay with her and work with Johnny roofing in Huston, Texas. My mom did not mind because I was doing nothing as far as work, she also thought that would be a good ideal. I called up my sister she asked Johnny if I could move in and work with him and James, he was the owner of his own roofing company that Johnny worked at. My sister called back later and it was ok to come. I had enough money to buy a bus ticket to Orange, Texas.

I went over Debbie's house very excited with the great news. We planned that I would move to Texas, work a few months to save money so I could purchase a plane ticket to fly back to California and enough money to pay for both of us to fly back to Texas. We hoped her parents would allow us to marry. This was a long shot but we were willing to take this leap.

So that was the plan. Of course I was very sad and so was Debbie, the thought of us being apart for this period of time. But we knew this was the only way it could work. We were to take one step at a time. We did not even know if her parents would laugh in our faces if we present them with our plans or not, but we would cross that bridge when we got to it.

I bought a bus ticket to Texas, loaded everything I thought I would need into a marine duffle bag and headed to Texas. This trip by Greyhound Bus was going to be at least a three day journey. These buses stop at every nook and cranny town along the way on interstate 10.

Once I arrived in Orange Texas, now remember this is January 1973 and I have entered into one of the most hick towns in Texas real Louisiana border and I had long hair carrying duffel bag with patches on my Levi jacket, I truly look like a hippy and I was very much out of place here and stuck out like a sore thumb. I called me sister's house, she was supposed to pick me up at the bus station, I waited for about an hour. No sister, so I called her house and no answer. So I thought to myself this is great, how am I going to get to her house and where is it at? I bought a map and found on the map where Orangefield was at. It did not look too far but certainly not within walking distance. So I start hitch hiking. I remember cars driving by and people yelling at me calling my name and I knew that I needed to catch a ride or something. I was feeling very uncomfortable and little threatened. Finally this ranchero pulls up to the curb. The guy, this big hick cowboy, asked where I was going and that I didn't look like I was from around there! I told him I was coming to visit my sister Donna Wallace, she lives in Orangefield and that's where I'm going.

He said, *"I know her, she does live there. She lives at the end of town by the cotton field"*. He said he needed to stop at this friend's house along the way for a minute and then he would drop me off at my sister's house. I started thinking how does this guy know my sister? So he pulls up in this drive way and started talking to this guy in a pickup truck and then he got back into his car and we took off driving towards Orangefield; I'm looking at the streets and kind of had an idea where she lived. I said, *"She lived off the main highway and we were on it, I believe she lives right there."* Because I could see the name "Wallace" on the mail box! As he passes my sister's driveway, I said, *"Hey let me out, that is her house!"* He said, *"No, that is not her house."*

Now I'm getting a little uncomfortable. I looked in the rearview mirror and I see this truck behind us, the same one that was at his buddy's house. Now this guy is not listening to me when I said *"Let me out of this car."* We seem to be driving around in some sort of a circle because we are now at the point of coming around by my sister's house again. And he is driving faster than before. So I thought to myself I need to get out of this car, now.

So as he slows down to make the turn in front of my sister's street, I open the door and jump out of his car. I hit the gravel road with a tremendous force; I was lucky I did not break some bones. He slammed on his brakes as I'm standing up to walk over to his car to retrieve my duffel bag from the back of his bed. He said *"What are you doing you could have killed yourself?"* I had said, *"Let me out and he refused to stop and to just leave me alone and get out of here."*

I walked over to my sister's driveway and waited until she got home. It was no more than an hour her and Johnny pulled up in his pickup truck and I was so happy to see her and him, what a relief!

Now let me give you a little back ground on Johnny. He is short, about my height 5'4" at best, very stocky and has an attitude, thinks he's better than anyone else and hates hippies or long hair, whichever. Right off the bat he starts giving me trouble, he said first the hair has to go, of course that's not going to happen if I could help it.

I remember one afternoon a couple of days after I got there, Johnny had this horse in a corral around back. He said, *"Dale get up on this horse."* I did not know this horse and had never ridden before, I just remember getting up on the horse and the next thing I know, I'm flying through the air and landed on my head. Oh I was knocked out for a little bit and my head was hurting so bad, of course he thought it was very funny.

I started working with him and James. The way you got paid was how many bundles of shingles you laid in a day; this was determined by the bands from the bundles that you kept and count them at the end of the day.

I wrote to Debbie every day and I also would go down the street from Donna's house, there was a little store and a telephone booth next to it. I would go to the store to get a few dollars in dimes and quarters and call Debbie every night. It was so wonderful to hear her voice, everything else was meaningless.

I do remember on a few occasions Johnny would try to be funny and push me off of some of the roofs just to entertain himself. One day he pushed the limit with me. We were at a job site in Houston and it was at lunch time, he found this rattlesnake and through it into the bed of the pick-up truck. He walked over to me and grabbed me. I stared fighting him and a few others came over and said let him give me a haircut because they do not like long hair. One of them grabbed a pair of tin snips while the other held me down and he proceeded to cut my hair off, then they through me into the back of the pick-up truck. I could hear the rattler making noise. I jump out of the bed almost as fast as I was thrown in there.

I started walking down the road yelling and cussing at them; James jumped into his truck and tracked me down. James did not participate in the hair cutting, I believe he was on the other side of the work site and did not know what was going on at the time.

He said, "*Dale get in the truck, I don't know what is the matter with these guys, but I sure am sorry and this will never happen again. I will talk to Johnny and let him know that this will never happen on my job site again, I will not put up with this type of behavior.*"

Of course things seemed to get a bit easier for me now that my hair is pretty short and I was forced to go and get my hair shaped up a bit so it would look half way descent.

About a couple of months later I had enough money to do what Debbie and I talked about doing. So I told my boss and sister that I wanted take a couple of weeks off and go see Debbie, which was not a problem at all.

After I took off work and return to California to see Debbie, I told her we could get married and move to Texas. Debbie was very excited with that thought as we talked about marriage on numerous occasions.

11

She was a little afraid of how her mom would react to such a shocking ideal that we had. She said, *"Dale you will need to ask my mother, I cannot do it."* She was a little afraid, and so was I. I said that I will come by tomorrow while you are in school and would simply ask for Debbie's hand in marriage and go back to Texas with me since I had a good job and we were so much in love with each other and we knew that we needed not ever be apart again.

So the following day I hitched a ride early in the morning to Debbie's house to have a talk with her mother. As I walked up the driveway I started to get so excited and afraid at the same time, I was an emotional roller coaster. As I knocked on the door, this was Wednesday, April 4th, her mother was surprised to see me and a bit confused, she knew as I did that Debbie was at school and being late morning. I remember she let me in and I said, *"Alice I need to talk to you about something that is on Debbie's and my mind for some time."* I said to Alice that I have a very good job now and I would like to have Debbie's hand in marriage and go back to Texas with me.

She was speechless for what seemed to be a long time. Then she said if me and Debbie really want to get married then that was fine as long as my mom was ok with that. I never even took to asking my mom but I knew that she would not give me any trouble. So I waited around hanging out with Alice and we waited for Debbie to come home from school. When Debbie walks in the door she was a little apprentice of what was going on. I said Debbie we are going to get married! She had a glow and a smile. Her mom said *"We will drive to Las Vegas this Saturday and we, will get you two married."*

We did have a slight problem, Debbie was only fourteen and I was seventeen. So we got out our birth certificates and we changed our years of birth so Debbie was sixteen and I was eighteen because in the state of Nevada a girl with parent signature can be married at the age of sixteen and a boy can marry at the age of eighteen with parent signature.

So later that evening I went home and told my mother that we were driving to Las Vegas this Saturday with Alice and Jim because Debbie and I are to be married. Of course she disagreed with it but I told her if she would not sign the marriage license I will have someone else sign for her. I did not care at this point. Nothing was going to prevent this marriage from happening.

In the meantime, I had the money to purchase two- one way airline tickets to Pasadena Texas, this is where Debbie's aunts Joy and Francis lived and we were planning on visiting them for a few days or a week pending on what we decided to do, before going to Orange field Texas where I was living with my sister Donna and her husband Johnny.

Come Saturday April seventh, 1973, first thing in the morning my mom, Alice, Jim, me and Debbie headed off to Las Vegas from her South Whittier home in Jim's dark blue Chevy station wagon.

Once arriving in Las Vegas we went to the Clark county court house to their marriage office that was open all night. Along with our parents and the justice of the peace, we were married that evening. I remember how beautiful Debbie looked in the yellow dress and her hair up in a bun like she had it in our pictures; she was so delightful to look at.

Our flight was leaving the morning of April 8, so we thought we would try to pull a fast one and go into the 4 Queen's Casino until they would catch us, but unfortunately we were stopped at the door, face it she was fourteen and looked it.

So we decided to just go to the airport and wait till morning, at least Alice, Jim and my mom could do a little gambling there. The next morning we boarded the flight to Texas. Her Aunt Frances picked us up at the airport and took us to her house in Pasadena. We spent a few days there. I remember we went to the "Alamo." I believe the Pasadena Zoo and we did a little fishing as well as going to one of those large flea markets. We were enjoying our time. We felt so "free" and independent, we were so relieved that now we are finally together.

Well it was time for us to go Orangefield so I could return to work. I believe I called my sister and told her that Debbie and I got married while I was in California. While I was staying at my sister's house I had my own bedroom so I could not think of any reason there would be any disapproval. But apparently Johnny disapproved and started giving me a hard time when we arrived at their house. Sometimes after work and he had a few to many Jax beers, Johnny would physically pick fights on many occasions with me in front of Debbie and of course upset her and was wondering what we got ourselves into. Me and Johnny would pretty much mess up the living room by fighting and my sister would get upset, but she had no control over Johnny; he was such a very arrogant person he had a short mans complex, but I was about the same height but only weighed maybe 110 soaking wet, and he was very stocky built but still short.

On the work job he would intentionally try to push me off the roofs of some of the houses we worked on, and he succeeded telling me how he   was   not   very   a   nice   person. So I knew it worried Debbie a lot and we did not have a car or did I have driver's license, but we knew that we needed to move from my sister's house. Fortunately Johnny was partners with this guy named James and he could not understand Johnny's behavior. Debbie tried to look for a place to live. No one would rent to us because of our age.

Then my sister said that Johnny's mom had a single wide trailer that was empty and needed to rent it out. This trailer was in Vidor, Texas out in the sticks and the only person on the property was another trailer that Johnny's mother lived in. So we moved and we were very happy to be in our own place finally. Debbie cleaned up the trailer and made it a home for us plus Debbie was a very good cook. I believe she was cooking for her family at the age of eight.

I believe we lived there for about a few months and Johnny's mom and her husband drank a lot of beer, things got a little uncomfortable so we moved to Port Arthur, Texas. James still came to pick me up every morning, he was a great guy. After a while we were invited to his house for dinner. His wife and Debbie, they got along very well.

Still Debbie and I got home sick for California. I called James up one day and asked if he would take me and Debbie to the Greyhound Bus station, but please don't say anything to my sister and Johnny, we just wanted to go home.

I believe it was late October 1973 when we boarded the Greyhound bus, it sure was a long time traveling in those days; the bus would stop at almost every little town. I do remember during our trip Debbie at one of the stops she ate spaghetti and cantaloupe, this did not agree with her stomach and she got sick on the bus, these buses only had one restroom in the back of the bus. Debbie said I think I'm getting sick so she went to the restroom; it seemed like a long time. When she came back to her seat she said don't go in there for a while. Trust me she was right, when I went into the restroom it smelt like vomit very bad, the smell lingered all night and most of the next day. Once we returned to California we stayed at her mom and Dad's until I found a job, still no car. I needed money to buy a car and I really had not driven much.

So all of my job hunting was by foot, it did not take me long to find a job. I was a gas station attendant for a Mobil gas station in La Mirada at the corner of Valley View and Imperial. It was about I would say 2-3 miles away, was not as bad as it could have been. I would walk to work and walk home in the evening. We worked long hours so I went to work in the dark and came home in the dark.

In the meantime after a few pay checks, Debbie started looking for a place to live. Well she found one. Her mother worked at bar called Little Henry's. Above Little Henry's was an empty apartment. It was large, had three bedrooms and so we jumped on it and moved in. unfortunately for me it added about another 1.5 miles to my walk to work.

We moved in to this apartment on top of a bar, there was only stair going up to the apartment on the back side of the bar and most of the times when we would come home there would be people sitting and drinking on our stairs, we would just excuse ourselves and walk on by. One of the most interesting things about where we lived was a big empty field behind. This homeless group of people lived there, around nine people or more. They called it "Potter's Field."

We got to know them pretty well, they were very friendly. They would build fires in the evening and sometime me and Debbie would stop and visit with them. We did not have much furniture so we had lawn chairs for the living room and from the customers from the bar leaving their empty glasses of beer we would check to see every now and then and pick up the empty glasses. On the evening when Debbie's mom worked, I could take out the bottom drawer and see into the bar, so we had a system. I would drop a rope and her mother would tie on a six pack of beer for me and I would pull it up.

There was one rule we needed to follow: during the day time we could not use the bath tub because it leaked onto the bar stools. We got used to the loud music playing from the juke box. It would finally quiet down around midnight.

I do remember in the morning going to work, there were so many stray dogs that would always come at me but fortune for me I never got bitten.

We lived there for about six months and we were ready for a more quitter location.

Debbie's uncle Johnny lived about ½ a mile from her dad's house on Crewe Street and the house behind him and his family became available to rent. It was a nice house with a good size yard.

So Debbie said lets rent this house and move, I said ok. The next day while I was at work, I started thinking maybe it's not a good idea to move. So later in the day I called Debbie and said I really don't want to move. She said sorry to me and her uncles moved us already, so you have a brand new place to live. That was just like Debbie, determined. She set her mind to do something and she drove forward to make it happen.

Once I got home later that evening I knew that Debbie's decisions usually are spot on. Besides, this was maybe a mile closer to my work. So while we lived in this house, both of us loved animals. We had a rabbit that was house broken; it used the cat litter box. I remember the rabbit would get up on the back of the coach and lay it's head on our shoulders. We also had a duck that was my drinking partner. On weekends I remembered giving the duck straight vodka, the duck loved vodka. We also had a chicken that would follow me to the mail box to retrieve our mail. And of course having her uncle Johnny living in the house next to us was always entertaining, he was the short uncle she had, he was 6ft 4in and about 260lbs all muscle.

While I was still walking to work to the gas station, Rudy who I work with had a Dodge Dart 1962 white car for sale for $100. Even though I still was a little afraid of driving, I bought the car and had Rudy drive it to my house.

I would take it out on the side streets and two blocks to her dad's house and back. I remember I would drive so slowly and Debbie would tease me and say "*DALE there is a cop behind you*" trying to freak me out and of course she would start laughing.

I believe the year was early 1974 and we moved just down the street from Debbie's dad on Hastings Dr. It was a two bedroom house and was even closer to my job.

And then Debbie became pregnant, we were going to have our first child. Debbie was so excited; she was going to be a mother. She started going to the clinic and I believe there were four rotating doctors, so she saw a different one each time.

Eventually I did go down and get my driver's license.

One evening Uncle Johnny wanted to know if I wanted to apply for a job where he worked.

I asked Johnny what kind of work is it and he said it is a steel fabricating company, called Horgren Steel, in Downey, CA. I was a bit concerned of the risk changing jobs since I work at the gas station for at least a year and I was in a comfort zone. But my thought was the possibility of making more money since Debbie and I were going to be parents.

I went for a job interview; I had no experience at all with steel work. The owner was Joe Horgren and this was a very small steel company, and he had seen the excitement I had of the possibility of a new job and it was for more money, I believe it was $2.60 per hour, and I was making $1.90 an hour at the gas station He also likes Uncle Johnny very much and so he hired me as a helper for the welders. First thing in the morning I would vacuum the offices, empty the trash, and clean the restroom. Then I went out on the floor as a welder's helper.

Debbie and I lived from pay check to pay check, but we were so care free and as long as the bills were paid, Debbie and I were happy, we lived off of what was left.

Ok, so now I have a new job, Debbie is getting into her sixth month of her pregnancy, I remember Debbie saying the baby has a strong heart beet at least that what the nurses were saying to her.

I started feeling more adjusted to my new job. I remember one afternoon, during Debbie's 8 month of pregnancy I got a call from Debbie, she was crying on the phone and said something was wrong with the baby and I needed to come home as soon as possible.

I got home and Debbie was at her dad's house up the street. She said that they cannot find or hear the baby heartbeat. She had an appointment in the morning to go back in the morning and have some fluids sample drawn from around the baby. I remember going in with her and she was lying on the table bed and they had this long needle sticking her in the stomach trying to find fluids. I remember Debbie crying telling them to stop it hurt too much.

I don't believe they ever did an ultrasound, we were so scared. Then they told us that she was never pregnant, that she had an unusual growth; I'm not sure what it is called but it starts out like a pregnancy but turns into this growth. What we could not understand is why these doctors let her go all the way to the eighth month before this was detected, and strange thing was all of her medical records disappeared from the clinic. She had to be submitted into the hospital and had this growth removed.

We were scared and very young, with no direction and should have sued this clinic, but we just wanted this all to go away.

We continued on with our life hanging out at Jim's house, it was a big family. Debbie's mom, dad, sisters, and their families were always popping in her uncle's house. There was always something going on at the Leonard's house.

We hung out with a lot of old friends like Jack Weaver, Robert Cummins, they all still lived in Bell Gardens and we would drive over and party a bit and then drive back to Whittier. This was getting a bit old; we wanted to be closer to our friends so we talked about moving over to Bell Gardens

So one day my friend Jack Weaver's mother had a house she was living in and behind her house was two rental houses that were connected. It was not any further from my job then it was from So Whittier just coming from the other direction. Jack, he lived in the garage next to the two houses behind his mother's house. I had purchased a 1965 Dodge Dart GT automatic push button transmission. Debbie still did not have her driver license, so we decide that she should go to driving school. After she got her driver license we needed to get another car because Debbie was getting a bit bored. She started looking for a job so I bought this Dotson pick-up truck, baby blue with a 289 mustang engine, this was cool. So Debbie landed a job at the same Taco Bell I was working at before we got married. This is where she met Karen Laible, she and her husband Gary Laible had moved to California from Niagara Falls NY, To attend college because of the cost, it was very cheap here in California verse NY. Karen and Debbie hit it off right away and became very good friends. We generally had had friends over every Friday and Saturday night, a regular group, Robert and Anita, Gary and Karen, Mike Bozik and whoever else decide to show up, like Jack's uncle Jocko.

We spent a lot of time in Jack's garage because he had a pool table in there and we play on it all the time. Listing to music and drinking beer was our normal social event.

Of course Jack's mom Fay was always keeping an eye on us, making sure we did not get out of hand back there. We had so much entertainment you never quite knew what the nights were going to bring.

I remember one night around 11:00 pm we all were watching a TV program, must have been about eight friends still at our house. And there is a knock on the door. I get up to answer the door and here stands this" hooker", and I said *"Can I help you?"* and she said, *"I don't suppose you called for me, right."* I said *"No, no one here called."* she said, *"ok can I come in and us you phone?"* I said ok so she came in and called up her man and then she left.

We were looking at each other like "what was that all about." Then another knock on the door and it was these two young kids from on the other side of the fence, laughing and said *"We just want to see what a hooker looks like so we called one up and sent her to your house so we could watch her."* I said you guys are BAD. And then they left, these two boys would always be doing something. I remember on Halloween night they made this dummy, it was full size of a man and they would hide on the side of a parked car and when they saw a car coming down the street they would throw this dummy over the parked car into the street and see how the people reacted driving, swerving out of the way of this dummy.

I remember one day Debbie and Karen were looking in the newspaper and they saw an ad for extras for a film that was going to be made with Bette Midler called "The Rose"
So these ladies went to the arena and were use as part of the audience for the film and they received a check for their time participating in this film.

After a while of living at this place, Fay, Jack's mom was going to move because the property was going into foreclosure, and we said we need to move and find another place to live.

There was a duplex on Jabonaria down the street, next to Robert's mom and dad that became vacant. So we moved into the duplex next to Robert's mom and Dad, Ed and Elsie. Our friends Karen and Gary moved into our old house to see how long they could go without paying any rent. The Dodge Dart we had was giving us trouble, electrical problems, so I bought Debbie a used 1963 red Ford Falcon, she fell in love with this car.

Now we have a lot of friends dropping in to visit and we enjoyed all of our friends very much, never a dual moment. Debbie and I would clean house every Friday after work and our friends would start coming in around 7:00 or 8:00 pm and we would buy beer; listen to music, and chat. We had a spare bedroom upstairs and we turned it into our art room. Gary Laible and I were always drawing or painting; we were getting into the "art" pretty deep and were enjoying every bit of it.

During this time my brother and Jennie had moved to Iowa. Debbie and I were planning on going out on vacation to visit them. While we were making our plans, my brother was in the process of trying to locate our father, who lived in Illinois at one time. Well low and behold he relocated him, in Clay City IL. My brother called me up and said, *"Dale I found our father and I spoke to him and he wants to see us."*

So let me give you a little history about my father. He left my mom when I was three years old and I never knew if he was alive or dead until my brother found him. I had mixed feeling about this, but yet I was still excited to see him.

Debbie and I flew to Iowa to my brother's house and the four of us drove to my dad's house in Clay City, it was about an eight hour drive. He was re-married to Ann; they've been together for at least fifteen years. Of course my dad really was glad to see me and my brother; they welcomed us with open arms.

I did ask my father why he left and he did say my mom was a bit on the wild side and very uncontrollable. She likes to go out a lot and I think he felt she was not "faithful."

But that still did not help my inner feelings why he never tried to stay in contact with us kids and I really was uncomfortable about asking him, so I just let go.

My step mom raised puddles and they had some pups and of course Debbie fell in love with this spotted black and white dog. Ann and my Dad gave it to Debbie I could not say no, Debbie really wanted this dog. After a few days at my dad's house we drove back to my brother's house. We took the dog and flew back to California. My wife named the dog "Oodles" the poodle.

This dog and I became enemies, this dog would poop in my house shoes if I left them out and paper or drawings out that the dog could get too, she would tear to shreds. This dog would walk right behind Debbie everywhere she went, like she was her tail.

I use to make the dog sit in the corner of the wall staring at it if she was being bad. I and the dog did not have a good relationship.

I do believe we ended up getting rid of this dog after Debbie started needing to lock the dog up in our bedroom when we both were working, especially after one weekend when Debbie spent the entire day making curtains for our bedroom. I remember coming home and as I was walking up to our duplex I could hear the dog howling and as I looked up to our bedroom there were no curtains hanging.

I proceed into the house and went upstairs and opened the bedroom door and this dog had destroyed our bedroom: ripped the curtains up, pooped all over the bedroom, taken all of our clean laundry that was in the basket and chewed most of my clothes up.

We felt that this could not continue so we needed to find a new home for this dog, and that was fine with me.

Probably, within six months my brother and Jennie moved back to California, I believe they moved in with Joe and Julie.

During these times we were very much into camping. We would all get together and plan camping trips, our main group was mostly just guys, me, my brother, Gary Laible, and Jack Weaver sometimes and a few other guys sometimes. When we went with our wives it was: Gary and Karen, Bill and Jennie, me and Debbie and Joe and Julie, Joe and Julie were Jennie's mom and dad. I remember we would go to Calico ghost town. They had a great camping site there. Or the guys would go to the Mojave Desert and spend the weekend, we always had a blast.

Sometimes we had a "treat", Joe and Julie would invite me and Debbie to go with them and Bill and Jennie in the motorhome. We felt we were in "style", no sleeping in a tent and on the ground.
I remember sitting around a camp fire at night drinking beer and just having a good old time chatting, laughing, and enjoying life to its fullest.

We all were so very close to each other, true friends, no bickering. If something was said that was taken wrong we always settled it and went on with our friendships.
Back in the seventies Disco dancing was in and we went out a lot with Bill and Jeannie to the Mississippi Moonshine Company in Downey, or we would get a group together and go to Pasadena to the Ice House, it was a place for comedians and live entertainment. A lot of times there were special guests. One night it was Lilly Tomlin, and as we were watching her, standing next to me was Pat Paulson, I am not sure if anyone remembers back in the early seventies (Pat Paulson for President)

Debbie and Karen on the other hand were "rebel rousers." Those two were going to take over the world, they made a stand at Taco Bell, and they refused to wear the uniforms that were given to them. They were very independent and smart; they would have the local drunks clean up the parking lot at Taco Bell for them so neither one of them had to do it. They would give the local drunks Taco Bell food in return for their, "job well done."

After Debbie and Karen left Taco Bell, they would go out looking for work as a pair. I remember them going in to a company called Elco Hillcrest and applying for work and apparently the owner was so impressed with the way these two young ladies preceded themselves that he hired them on the spot and put them both in charge of this company heading up most of the employees, most of them were Spanish speaking women.

We went to my dad's house on our next vacation. By this time we were getting along real good with them. Debbie and Ann were talking quite often on the phone so when we flew to see them, and down the street from them was this little empty house and it had been empty for years. Now these houses on this dirt road were built during the oil booming days in the fifties, and this one in particular was abandoned. So Ann said she would look into it to see if it could be bought. But we were in no hurry so we stayed at their house for a week. We went and saw my aunt Unajean and uncle Kunene, we also went to this old village called New Harmony built in the 1700's, we had a wonderful stay but had to get back home.

After returning home my work at Horgren Steel was coming to an end. One morning I went to work and the doors were lock. The company went belly up, and he went out of business. I was very thankful for a lot of years, I believe I worked there for five years. Being very educated in the steel industry, I worked my way up it the company from a janitor to a welder's helper and painter, and was being trained to become a burner, cutting steel with a torch machine. Joe Horavat was the owner. He gave me a lot of opportunities for growth within the company. Debbie's uncle Johnny and I were quite a team at that company. But all good things come to an end.

During this time my step mom and my dad wanted us to move to Illinois to the house down the street from them. I called and said we could buy the house for back taxes of $240.00, we thought what a buy. So we sold what we could, and gave a lot away and stayed with Debbie's mom and dad for a couple of weeks until we were able to get everything in order for our adventure. We were feeling a bit displaced and needed a change.

I still had the little pick-up truck and I bought a camper shell to put on this truck.

I remember it was around September of 1978 and I was working on getting the truck ready for our trip and I remember the engine was running a little hot so I decided to leave out the thermostat so the truck would run cooler, what a mistake that was.

We loaded all of our clothes, my albums and record player and what we felt we still wanted to keep but only what we could fit in the back of this truck. I remember I had a lift kit on the rear end and it was bottoming out. We headed east.

I remember this truck was modified to fit this 289 engine in this little Dotson truck and I had a lot of drafts coming in here and there around the floor board.

I believe our first day we were on route 66 heading to Kingman, Arizona and I started hearing this high pitch sound coming from my engine, we stopped at this gas station in Kingman and popped open the hood and it was the pulling on the alternator. The attendant said that he could not fix it but it would get me to the next town. So we start heading on the highway, got about five miles out of Kingman and started smelling smoke so I pulled over to the side of the road and popped open the hood and the pulley had frozen up and the belt was slipping on the pulley.

Lucky I had a CB radio in the truck and was able to call and have a tow truck come and tow us back to Kingman.

I had him take us to the station where we were earlier because I noticed next to the station was a motel. The attendant said it would take a couple of days to get a new or rebuilt alternator, so we just hung out at the hotel and around town until my truck was fixed.

Once the truck was fixed we headed east again. I remember stopping in Gallup, New Mexico that evening and the weather was getting chilly. So we stop at this hotel and spent the night and back in those day you could put a quarter in this machine and the bed would vibrate you to sleep.

Well the next morning there was a frost over everything and my truck was not warming up very good, really not all. So I need to remove the frost of course I did not own a ice scraper, so I went back to the room and got a bucket of warm water thinking it would melt the ice on the windshield. I poured the warm water over the windshield and it froze instantly.

So I look in the back and found a pair of scissors and proceed to scrap off the ice. I was able to make a small hole about 10" in diameter to see out of to drive, and by doing so I scratched the glass pretty bad. But we were now on our way leaving Gallup, New Mexico.

As the sun started to rise, the heat from the sun started melting the ice on the windshield. The temperature was still very cold and we needed to keep our coats on because the heater was not warming up very well

24

and a lot of drafts were coming in around the center console. We were still excited about this adventure even with the discomfort from the cold.

I do remember old route 66 went right through Santa Fe, New Mexico. We stopped at the little Mexican restaurant; they had the best breakfast burritos I ever had. While sitting there I noticed all of these photographs on the wall. I walk over to see them and they were of famous people like John Wayne, Roy Clark in front of this little restaurant. This must have been a stopping place for celebrities along this route.

We got back in our truck and continue on our journey. As we headed north east, the weather was getting worse and it was snowing a bit. I can't remember where we stopped that night, but the next morning it was snowing quite heavy.

This was going to be our last day on the road and we were very antsy to get to my dad's. The snow was making it hard to drive at a reasonable speed to make so good time, so as the sun started to set, the snow fall was getting very heavy and hard to see the road. I stopped at this little hotel restaurant – bar to see if we could have a room for the night, I was wore-out from the drive. They had no rooms available, so I used the phone booth and called my dad and I told him where we were and he said we were only about fifty miles away.

We headed back on the road. That last fifty miles seemed like two hundred miles, it took forever to get there. We were so cold in the cab of this truck that with all of the draft coming in my Levis pants leg was frozen and had frost over them.

What a relief it was to pull into his driveway and get into a warm house. Well the next day we walk up the road, no more than five hundred feet to our new home that we bought for $250.00 back taxes. We went in and we saw the possibility of a really cozy home. We had quite a bit of money saved so we decided we would go down and start buying supplies like paneling for the walls, paint, and the roof leaked as well. I went to turn on the water and the water leaks came from everywhere under the house. So now this is going to be another challenge. But in the mean time I need to look for work. I must have gone to everyplace within a fifty miles radius, from steel company to oil rigs. No one was hiring. I did not give up. I still reviewed the newspaper every day and still made time to work on the house. Debbie and my step mom and dad were helping in every way and every day. I believe it took me three days to complete the re-roofing, this at least stopped all the drips through the ceilings.'

Once the house was complete and we finally moved about two months later, I was still concerned because I was still not working. Than Debbie started getting real sick could not keep anything down and was very dehydrated. We ended up going to the doctor and they admitted her to the hospital. And this is when we discovered she was pregnant. I believe she was in the hospital for about a week. Once she came home to our house, we did a lot of soul searching. We wanted to stay here, but without employment it would be very risky. I knew it would crush my dad and step mom, if we decided to leave and head back west to California. They worked so hard to help us make this home possible. But I needed to think what is the most logical decision to make and with Debbie in this condition we made the decision to go back to California.

I called up my step mom and dad and said, "*I cannot find work and Debbie is going to have our child, I feel its best we go back to California because I know I can get work there.*"
Clay City was out in the middle of "nowhere", the closest town is Flora and that was at least thirty to forty miles away. They were a bit upset but this is our decision.

So I was thinking what a horrible drive it was coming here and I did not want Debbie to endure this trip again.

I called up my brother up and I said, "*Bill if I pay for your ticket to fly to St Louis airport, will you help me drive back to California?*" I would drive to St Louis and put Debbie on an airplane and wait around and pick up my brother. So we arranged her flight out with an hour of my brother's flight coming in. St Louis was only a three to four hour drive from Clay City if we decided to leave and head back west to California. And before we left Clay City I went down and purchased a thermostat so the truck temperature would heat up so the cab could get warm.

I remember loading up the truck, Debbie was helping me and we were sad, but yet glad to be going home and the snow and the bitter cold here was just a little too much of us to take.

So we drove to the airport, I was so glad Debbie was not going to have to endure this long drive home with me. I walked her to her departing gate and I waited for my brother. Once he arrived we hit the road. Driving all night and all day, we stopped for a while at this little hotel and lie down for a couple of hours and hit the road again.

Once we arrived back in South Whittier, Debbie was waiting, what a sight for sore eyes she was.

Ok now we needed to get real serious. Debbie is pregnant and I needed a job, we were only planning to stay with her parents for a short time. During this time Debbie's mom seemed to be very unhappy with her life, she would disappear at the drop of the hat and go to Oklahoma without saying anything or say anything to anyone. I believe she was looking for something new. I knew this was hurting Jim very much, and Brenda was either eleven or twelve years old. Debbie was very concerned about someone looking after Brenda since their mother seemed not to be very concerned when she would leave and return when she was ready. She would be gone for weeks and all of a sudden she would come back like nothing was wrong. We all were a bit confused with this type of behavior she displayed.

So, I went over to this steel company that I saw awhile back when we lived here before. It was Riverside Steel; they made large gutter beams for high rise construction buildings.

I applied for any job preferably a fitter job. The pay was much better than a helper, but of course the only opening was a welder's helper job, so I took it.

After a while we were able to save enough money to look for a house of our own again, so we called up our old landlord that we had and she was so sad when we moved before, she had said if we ever needed to rent a house to give her a call. So we did and there was a house right next to the previous house we moved out of on Hastings Dr.

This was great. So we moved into the house and one day I was over at Jack Weavers in Bell Gardens and he said that he was renting a house in South Whittier, and we asked where, and he said on Crewe St. this was the same street Debbie's Dad lived on, this is a short street Crewe St. dead end into Hasting St. So, low and behold Jack was moving about four houses down from us now, weird part is that he was living with Lori.

By this time Debbie had a real doctor to look after her during this pregnancy. I have a job and we are happy again, really no worries just waiting on our new arrival. Until one afternoon, I believe it was in the early part of Debbie's pregnancy, Jim was driving his Simi on the General Motors lot and there was this blind side along the railroad track without any indicating warning lights of oncoming trains and his trailer was hit by a train and drug him down the tracks. He went to the hospital for observation and was released.

A couple of day later I believe it was from the trauma of the incident he had a heart attack, and was rushed to the hospital. I remember me and Debbie going up to the hospital and seeing Jim, he seemed ok and doctors reassured us he was going to be fine. We left the hospital and no later than we got home we received a call and James had died of a massive heart failure.

Debbie was so heartbroken and she was struggling so hard to cope with this loss of the only real caring parent she had, even if he was really not her biological father, Manual Morgan was her real father but that was still debatable. Now our son is due in about two months. Debbie was so depressed she could not even attend his funeral. I remember that I, Gary Laible, Jack Weaver and Lloyd were the pallbearers.

Debbie is now in her seventh month and we were taking the classes for child birth, I forget what they were called, the classes.

I remember when Debbie went into labor the night before we went to the hospital. We waited all night for her to dilate and it just was not the time. Early in the morning my brother called me up and said, *"Dale why don't you meet me for breakfast while you are waiting."* I told Debbie I was going to run and meet my brother and I will be back in about an hour. She said, *"Go, I will wait right here for you."* So I went to breakfast and when I returned to the hospital they were wheeling Debbie into the labor room, what luck I made it on time, if I missed this it would have been devastating.

Once I was in the delivery room I put on the gown and I was standing next to Debbie holding her hand and she had such a grip I thought she was going to break my fingers. I was watching the birth by looking into the mirror above Debbie's head; it was angled so you could see what the doctor was doing. Now by this time I was not too good with the sight of blood, and was getting a bit faint. The nurses asked, *"Are you ok Dale?"* Of course I was trying to compose myself, *"Yes I'm ok."*

Once Joshua came out on March seventh 1979 the doctor was concerned about the shape of his head and she told Debbie, *"Once I seen your husband, I noticed they both have the same head shape."* I was at ease knowing he was normal.

We brought Joshua Lee Weatherford home; Debbie was a very happy mother but still grieving over the loss of Jim. Well Alice decided to sell Jim's house and sell everything and move to Shawnee, Oklahoma, and take Brenda with her. Debbie was so concerned about the wellbeing of Brenda. She knew she could not stop her mom from leaving. So Debbie and I talked about if for some time and decided that we should move to Oklahoma so Debbie could keep an eye on Brenda. This is a big sacrifice for us but I understood Debbie's love for her little sister.

My job was fine but what the heck, let's do another move. So after Alice moved and got settled, her mom was happy that we were going to move to Oklahoma. We loaded up my little pick- up truck I still had and we also had a Chevy Vega. I drove the truck and Debbie and Jennie was in the Vega, it took about three days to get to Shawnee, Oklahoma. I remember driving down Main Street, Shawnee and was thinking oh my god this is such a hick town, what am I getting myself into here, work might be very scarce or scary?.

We arrived at Debbie's mom's house, it was a very nice house, old but nice. This very first night we were sitting on the front porch and the sirens started going off. Debbie looks over at her mom and asked *"What is that siren for?"* Her mom said. *"Oh it's just a tornado been sighted."* Debbie said let's get to the storm cellar! Debbie grabs Josh in her arms and we went to the cellar. The cellar was about a foot full of standing water so we grabbed some milk crates to stand on until we felt the storm had past.

Later that evening my sister-in-law, Jennie, was washing her hair in the kitchen sink and she felt something bump up against the back of her knees, she turned and looked to see it was one of the kitchen chairs. No one was in the room at that time but her. After she was done, she mentioned this incident to us and Alice said that there were a lot of strange things happening in this house that could not be explained.

So the next day we took Jennie to the airport and thanked her for helping Debbie and I with this journey.

As we settled in at Alice's house on Wallace Street, we lived just a couple of houses from the railroad tracks across the street from a little convenient store. I remember it was right in the middle of summer and the humidity was high, and Alice only had a wall mounted air conditioner in the living room. Debbie and I stayed in the front bedroom, which was a little larger than the other two bedrooms so we could have room for a crib for Joshua.

I really was not feeling good about this move but I knew deep in my heart that Debbie felt the need to come out to Shawnee. She felt she owed this to her father, Jim, to keep an eye on Brenda, to make sure she was being taken care of. I hate to say this but Alice was not or even close to being a perfect mother figure. So I knew that I needed to do my best. And the first thing I felt I needed to do was to find a job, even as bad as the economy was here in this small town.

I started looking for work and applied at Shawnee Steel, as a burner-fitter, they said they will review my application and get back to me. I did not feel that they would. But I really liked the set up there; they were into structural steel, right up my alley. My next stop I went and applied at Shawnee Mill, no luck there.

While driving, I spotted Belches Trailer Company; it was of course a manufacture of flatbed trailers, nothing intriguing for me. They hired me on the spot, I forget what the pay was at that time, and I think it was minimum wage. So I was very happy to land a job and went straight home to Debbie and told her of my splendid luck. She was so relieved, she was very worried that I was going to have a bit of trouble finding a job but now she was ok.

The next morning I went to work at Belcher Trailer, was not feeling like this was going to be right for me as the day wore on. Come lunch time I called Debbie and she said, "Shawnee Steel called and wanted to know when I could start", I was so excited they were no more than three or four miles from where I was, so I clocked out for lunch and drove over to Shawnee Steel and Arvin Kilgore was the shop manager and hired me on the spot, I believe it was for about $1.00 more a hour than what the trailer company was paying me.

Of course I could not past this up; I called Debbie and told her I have a new job already and more money.

So I quit the trailer company and started at Shawnee Steel the next morning. Arvin was this older gentleman, probably in his late fifties or early sixties, always had a large amount of chewing tobacco in his mouth, but very nice. He placed me in charge of all steel cutting using straight line burner or hand torches. The first few days were very good. The men I worked with were some of the best good ole boys you could ever meet.

Now that we were getting established in the area, Debbie wanted to do some part time work just to help out with the finances. She saw an ad for working at the "Roundhouse" Overalls Company.
She went and applied and the lady that interviewed her looked at her application and said, *"Your husband is Dale Weatherford?"* Debbie replied *"Yes"* the lady said, *"That cannot be true, Dale Weatherford is getting married to my daughter in a couple of weeks."*

Debbie said, *"Well I guess there must be another Dale Weatherford because we just moved here a few weeks ago."* She hired Debbie and Debbie thought it was so she could keep an eye on her. But of course if you knew Debbie, she always applied herself and always did her best and they soon found out she was a very valuable employee to their company.

We were feeling good. Our life was simple now, and we were not all wrapped up in that rat race like we were in California.

I remember back when we were asking Alice about the odd incident that happened to Jennie in the kitchen. Alice said, *"That almost every night in her room is this wind-up toy that would start going off for no reason at all in the middle of the night."* Another incident happened one night the weather was so hot that Brenda was sleeping in the living room. All of a sudden she started screaming and Brenda ran into our bedroom. Debbie said," Brenda what is the matter." Brenda said she was awake and she saw the rocking chair started rocking back a forth and you could hear it on the wooden floor. She thought it was the dog "spotty" that had jump up on the chair, and then she moved her leg and felt "spotty" curled up sleeping at the end of the couch.

This house had some bad vibes to it; I remember one afternoon Debbie and I was in our bedroom sitting on the bed just chatting. There were two doors leaving this bedroom, one into the living room and one door going onto the front porch. All of a sudden something from outside hit the door going to the front porch so hard it bent the latch that locked the door. We jumped from being startled. I rushed over to the door and opened it and the storm door on the outside was locked and the windows were closed. We could not figure out what caused this to happen; there was no wind and even if there was, all of the windows were closed and locked and the storm door was locked. This frightened us a bit, it was something unexplainable.

I remember on another occasion I was in the bathroom taking a bath. There was no shower in this house, and I preferred showers. I was sitting in the tub, the washer and dryer were in this bathroom as well, and as I glanced over to the washer there were two diaper baskets about twelve inches apart and as I watched in amazement as these two baskets slid up against each other all by themselves.
I quickly got out of the tub and was out of the bathroom as fast as I could.

I said to Debbie, *"You would not believe what just happen in the bathroom."* After that, things seem to calm down a bit.

Since I had a good job, Debbie starting looking for a house and found one on the other side of town, it was a two bedroom house with a good size yard. We were pretty happy living there, at least it was our own, and it's hard to live in someone else home.

Joshua was getting bigger and keeping us on the run he was about year and a half old. He was all "boy", had Debbie on her toes all the time. But we were not pleased with renting; we wanted to buy a house of our own. So after a while, about 6 months, we started looking for a house to buy.
Some distant cousin of Alice wanted to sell her house in Tecumseh, the next town over.
Debbie and I went over to see the house, it was a HUD house I believe, and we were first time buyers and we also was eligible to fall into the bracket to get a loan to buy this house. It was a three bedroom brick home with a two car garage.

These people were not the cleanest and the house had roaches and a lot of them. After we bought the house we set off so many smoke bombs, it took months to get rid of them. And of course Debbie was not going to put up with the nasty bugs.

The house was a brick home, 2 car garage, and a fence in back yard, the perfect place for us to settle down. Debbie wanted a garden so we chose an area in the corner of the yard and I went and borrowed a tiller. Little did I know that Oklahoma dirt was mostly red clay, and red clay is not good for growing vegetables.

We tried to add new soil and mix it with the clay; this still did not work out to good. Eventually we abandoned the task of creating a garden.

The people on our street were very laid back and we met a couple across the street Jim and Terry, they had a daughter name April and she was Joshua's age. Next to them was David and Sherry and their daughter was named Brandi. Next door to us was a fireman. He was single and kept to himself a lot, but he was a very nice person.

Debbie was still close enough to her mom in Shawnee; she could drive over there in a matter of twenty to thirty minutes.

I remember Debbie would go over her mom's house once a week to clean here house. Her mother did not pick up things and the house was a mess most of the time.

When James died of a heart attack, Alice received a good settlement check to avoid a law suit to General Motors, because actually the accident was on the GM property and it was due to improper warning signals to avoid these kinds of incidents. And she also collected his social security checks. She was sitting very well financially.

She also made a point that we were not to expect any financial help if we needed it, but Debbie and I never asked anything from anyone, we were always self-supporting and if we could not afford something, we did without. The only thing we were concerned about was taking care of Joshua and making sure our bills were paid.

My work was doing very well and I met this guy, Sam Deal, we became very close friends. He and his wife Janet were dropping by our house or we would go and visit them.

We all liked to go out on a Friday night or Saturday night and we would go to this place called "Cowtown", it was a bar with live music, dance floor, and quite big inside. So we would usually get a group together and head over there for a good night out.

Brenda was a teenager, so Debbie and I would have her watch Joshua at our house and in the morning either Debbie or I would take Brenda home. We were very particular about who we were leaving Joshua with, so Brenda was it.

We spoke about having more children and I talked her into having one more kid. I thought this would be good, Joshua is now two years old and it was the end of 1981. Low and behold, it did not take long and we were to be parents again. Debbie's second pregnancy, she was sick quite often. I helped Debbie with Joshua after work and sometime Brenda would come over on the weekends and help as well.

I remember we had a Jeep CJ7, and I felt that now we are going to be a little larger family we needed a bigger car. I had this hair brain ideal of trading in the jeep for this Chevy Chevette, Debbie disagreed very much. But of course I was thick headed and did it anyway. Debbie said, *"Ok, you will drive this car until it dies."* This was a lesson I will pay for years.

On September 16, 1982 Dylan Lee Weatherford came into our world, born at Shawnee Medical Center, Shawnee, OK. Very healthy baby boy, because that was another thing Debbie was always concerned about, was the wellbeing of her health. She was so concerned about her conditions during both pregnancies she was always thinking of what she was putting in to her system.

My job at Shawnee Steel was getting a bit boring, and Jim McDonald, across the street was into body shop repairs, buying cars that have been in accidents and fixing them up to sale. He did most of his work out of his garage. He had a good reputation around town. Jim and I became real good friends. He said to me one day, *"There is an empty shop on main street, why don't you and me go into business together, you can be your own boss and I have plenty of back log work we can make some real good money for both of us."*

I talked it over with Debbie and it was a gamble but we always were throwing the dice, that's how we roll. Debbie said go ahead and do it. I help Jim get the shop set up and he was working and I was working more so on the weekends until I felt comfortable in quitting Shawnee Steel.

Once I started working with Jim full time, we were working long hours and the money was not coming in like I thought it was going too, at least not for me because I more or less worked for him and he handled all the finances, so with our overhead there was not much left over, at least that was the indication I was led to believe. It was a struggle making money but I was determined to make it and we did.

Debbie was a genius when it came to juggling money and also she was very thrifty. I remember when she would go to garage sales. She would come home with all kinds of toys for the boys, they never went without, and she made sure of that! These two boys and I was her life and she was very happy with that, she never asked for anything we could not afford, she also put me and the boys first before herself.

So after Dylan was about one year old, we decided to go on a vacation to California in the little white Chevette. We bought a small storage roof mounting container and attached it to the roof of this car, loaded it up and went to California on a two week vacation.

The trip went flawless. We stayed at my brother's house in Norwalk. We were glad to be back home and were enjoying the surroundings. My brother was working at the company in Buena Park California called Certified Fabricators Inc. This was the largest aircraft tooling company west of the Mississippi. Seventy-five percent of the work being done there was for the space shuttle. This struck a nerve in me, my brother said, *"Dale why don't you go put in an application and see if they might be interested in hiring?"*

I spoke to Debbie about what my brother had said and Debbie thought that it would be nice to move back to California again.

The next day I drove over to CFI and applied for a job as a "fitter." I was interviewed right on the spot by Bob Stubbe, he was the fabrication manager. We spoke about how I was living in Oklahoma at the time, he had said they needed a fitter real bad and he could start me out at $5.50 per hour, working twelve hours a day and half day on Saturday. I felt like a kid in a candy store, this I felt would be my opportunity to advance from where I was, remember my goal in life was to be able to provide for my family solely on my income, my Debbie was to focus on raising our two boys, and taking care of me too.

I was a bit old fashion, I did not want Debbie to work I wanted her to live, to do what she wanted.

Speaking with Bob Stubbe I told him I would call him in the morning, I let him know that I still needed to go back to Oklahoma and work things out. He was fine with that but wanted me to start as soon as possible.

I came back to my brother's house and told Debbie I have a wonderful opportunity to advance and the potential to make some real "good money" with an aggressive motive, and a determined drive.

Debbie was fine and also excited, but we had some planning we needed to do. So vacation time here in California was over and we headed back to Oklahoma. Her concerns about Brenda were still the same. Brenda was a teenager and she pretty much was heading in her own direction.

Once we got back, Debbie and I thought long and hard on how we were going to make this happen.

We decided that I would fly to California live with my brother and start working at Certified Fabricators while she started packing and getting the house ready for sale.

This was the summer of 1984. Once I got to Certified Fabrications, Bob Stubbe said that the position I applied for was no long open so he started me out as a helper. This consists of grinding all day long, sometimes or painting tools, not what I was expecting. But I was allowed to work as many hours as I wanted too. So working seventy to eighty hours a week was giving me a lot more than we were used too.

Every evening Debbie and I would talk on the phone for hours, I really missed her and the boys, but I was given this opportunity and we both knew we had to do this no matter how painful it was for us at that time. I believe we were apart for about a month.

Once Debbie and the boys were ready to come out, I flew to Oklahoma and we all drove out to California. We stayed at my brother's house, could not of been more than a couple of weeks, then we found a nice house in uptown Whittier to rent. It was on a nice quite street. Debbie's arranged with her uncle Junior to drive out to California with our house belongings that were going in a trailer for us. He also had a house in northern California, so our new home was on the way to his house. I remember the night we were sitting in our newly empty rented house, I believe it was late in the evening when Debbie's uncle and aunt drove up to the house. I felt that it was all coming together for us once again.

We were back in sunny California and very happy to be reunited on our own again.

It has always has been hard for us to live with another family, even if it's only for a short period of time. Debbie and I were so dependent on each other it was like one soul that we were sharing.

It was a bit of a drive for me to get to work, but I was fine with that. The only thing that mattered to me was to make the family happy and to become a good provider. Working at Certified Fabricators I felt that this would take place in the industry. I put a lot of precious family time aside for my work, and that was not a good or logical decision, I know now.

I started forcing on, getting ahead in life. You see my education was limited and I had no degree, but I wanted to make as much money as possible. I did not want my family to want things they could not have, especially my Debbie, we both had a hard up bring.

I still continued to oil paint in my spare time; I joined the Whittier Art Association, and even had an art showing at one art gallery. Debbie still had her hands full with the boys. I got so consumed with work; I put my art aside and stopped painting altogether after a few months.

I'm not sure why but we decided to move back to South Whittier. I do believe we were more comfortable in that area of town and the drive was getting a bit old and Debbie was unhappy with the school district. We contacted our old landlord and she said that the house right next to the one we lived in on Hastings, before we went to Oklahoma was vacant, we thought that was great!

In the mean time I was talking to Jack and he said that he had rented a house in South Whittier on Crewe Street, and by coincidence that was the street Debbie's late dad Jim lived on and it also was the connecting street to Hastings Dr. That was a strange incident.

We move into our new house, about four houses down from Jack Weaver. Debbie and I would hang out at the house, Dylan was two years old and Joshua was five years old. We still went on camping trips with the usual crowd. We would go to Calico ghost town a lot to camp, we had plenty of fun and of course the boys enjoyed getting out in to the Desert.

We tried to go out some place at least a couple of times a month. Joshua Tree was another place we went quite often. I remember then that Debbie was having a bit of a problem with Joshua's school because it was bi-lingual and she felt he was not getting the proper education for the time he is in school, and Debbie wanted to go back to work, and further her education; just trying to find a direction besides staying at home. I remember my mom called us up one afternoon and said that Donna and her new husband were coming out to California for Christmas. But my mom was living in this very small trailer that could not have been longer than a single wide trailer; she just did not have the room for company.

So Debbie and I talked it over and said since Donna did help us when we first got married that we would volunteer to let them stay at our house. The week before Christmas, Donna and her new husband arrived. Debbie and I welcomed them into our home with open arms. We cleaned up one of the boy's room and let them stay in there and put both of the boys in the same room.

Debbie and I took them everywhere and paid for dinners. We did everything possible to make their stay enjoyable. Donna said to my mother that she ran out of cash and would she take a personal check for cash and take to her the bank, back then there was not a computer, so when a check was cashed it took sometimes a week to clear. My mom took Donna's check to the bank and cashed it for her. I believe it was for $500.00, back then that was a lot of money.

A couple of days later I was getting ready to go to the store and I was low on cash, I said in front of my sister and her husband, "*Debbie I need to go to the bank and get some money from the day and night teller , and what is our access code?*" She told me the code and I proceed to go out the door and Donna's husband said, "*Dale is it ok if I ride along with you?*"

Of course I said, "*Sure come on.*"

After I went to the bank and went to the store to get a few things, once we got back to the house and ate dinner Donna said that they needed to be going back to Texas in the morning. I asked, "*Do you need us to take to the airport?"* and she said, *"No you guys done enough for us we need to leave early in the morning so we will just call a cab."*

The next morning when we woke up, Donna and her husband were gone. It was a bit of a relief, no company to entertain; we can get back to our normal routine.

After a few days had passed Debbie asked, *"Dale have you seen my day and night teller card?"*

I said, *"No, I have my own card."* Debbie continued to dig in her purse and looking around the house. She started to get a little concerned that it was missing from her purse. So she called the bank to check on our bank account. Low and behold our bank account had been drained out. Debbie asked the lady at the bank where was this money taken out at and she said it was at a machine at LAX over a couple of days. You see back then you could only take out so much money per day and Donna and her husband stayed at the airport hotel until they emptied my account. Also the check Donna wrote to my mom bounced. So my mom had to make the check good and she was living on state funds. My mom barely had enough money to live on as it was. Of course it was Christmas time and all of our bills we had paid bounced due to no money in my account. This really put me and Debbie in a financial bind. I felt really bad because I left myself open. I really did not think twice about asking Debbie for our code for the bank in front of my sister, she was family.

We called my sister up and said, *"Donna why would you do this to us?"* And of course she denied it and after a while of Debbie drilling her she ended up admitting to it. We said you know Grace (my mom) trusted you. She cannot afford making your check go. Donna really did not care. So this was the time. We wrote my sister off and being part of our family. And of course my mom forgave Donna but Debbie and I would never trust her again, she really hurt us money wise.

We started getting that feeling that we needed to move on. We were tired of the area we were living in and it was getting to be a bit rough around this area of South Whittier, a lot of gang activity.

We started looking around the Norwalk area and found this house on Excelsior Avenue. It was right across the street from the elementary school. Great location, not too far from work and it was close to Cerritos

College, Debbie was interested in going back to school for medical training.

So this house was perfect, had a garage in the back it was three bedrooms and it looked really nice from the street. We moved in to the house but we noticed that the house next to us had some pit bulls in the yard and the fence between us and them was this old picked fence with some white paint on it and a few un-nailed slats. We did not give it to much attention at that time, we were glad to be moving again, as you can see Debbie and I enjoyed our new surrounding quite often.

Once we move in, to get to the garage or the back yard you needed to walk down the next driveway and this un-sure fence where these dogs ran along the other side of the driveway. There was so much junk in their yard that you could not see very well and we only thought there were one or two dogs.

Our back yard was surrounded by a six foot. cinder block wall, on the other side of the wall was the alley. There was a gate that opened up to the alley. I made sure that this gate was always locked.

I was, at first, not too concerned about these dogs until one day the family that lived in this house, these Mexican guys would tie a rope and have these dogs hang from the rope by their teeth to straighten their jaws. I started counting the dogs I would see and they had at least four or five dogs at a time. Now I'm worried about our kids, every now and then I would see one or two out of the yard, they would squeeze under the fence or dig a hole to get out. I went over to knock on their door many times telling them that their dogs were out of the yard. I was afraid they would hurt somebody or worst one of my kids or even my wife Debbie.

I had called animal control many times on these dogs and on the owner for not keeping them under control, and of course by the time animal control got there the dogs would be back in the yard, this battle went on for quite some time.

In the meantime, Debbie was very interested in going to college, and since Cerritos College was only a couple of miles away, I was all for Debbie going to school to further her education, she wanted to have a profession in the medical field. Debbie enrolled into a Medical assisting program at Cerritos College.

Debbie was the type of person that once she set her mine to accomplish something, she did, no matter what it took. Besides, Debbie had this personality that radiated from her that you just like being around her. Everybody found her very friendly and likeable, this is what made the medical field so attractive to her, she loved being around people. She could talk to a stranger on the street for hours, that is just how she was, I feel she was very gifted in that sense.

I remember during this time when she was going to college, she started getting headaches; she was taking aspirin for the headaches but after a while that stopped working.

She went to see her doctors and they really could not figure out what was going on. They put her on some pain pills, but the headache began to be more intense. After a few weeks, she started get to where she was sick to her stomach. The headaches were not stopping; they were turning in to migraines. The pain medication was increased to a stronger dose; it was making her so loopy she could not even drive.

I remember Debbie saying, that the doctors could not find anything wrong and they wanted her to start going to a clinic for learning how to live with the pain. I thought that's ridiculous. Debbie said that she needs to find another doctor and I agreed.

It took a while, but she did find another doctor she thought she could trust. She explained the situation and they did an x-ray on her nose passage, and discovered her sinus was undeveloped, this was causing pressure, and creating the headaches. So the doctor said they would need to do surgery to correct this problem.

At this point Debbie and I was so relieved that this most likely would correct the problem and she would not need to live with the amount of pain that she was in, I don't understand how someone would need to live with pain just because one doctor could not figure out the problem.

She was admitted to the hospital and the surgery was performed. The way they entered the sinus area was going in through the mouth cutting between the gum and the cheek to enter the sinuses and they cauterized the blood vessels and the arteries to relieve the pressure.

I worried about her as I always did. You see Debbie is such a unique person that when she has something going with her system, it generally is to the extreme. After the surgery her headaches went away and we went on with our normal life.

Debbie was also in many activities with the college and every year the college had a festival where before the home coming game they had a celebration, and each profession at the college would design a float with a theme pertaining to the class and of course Debbie in the medical field would design a float with reference to the class. I remember the first year Debbie volunteered me to help design a float. The theme was with Mickey Mouse and Minnie Mouse; mine was giving Mickey and injection on a table. So after work in the evening I would meet Debbie at the college and help design the float made from chicken wire and we inserted color paper to create the colors. It took about a couple of hours and hard work from the class of women and I to complete a float and we were very proud of our creation.

So this became a recital for years to come. I remember one afternoon I had come home from work and I received a call from Debbie's instructor and she had said that Debbie was sitting in class and all of a sudden her nose started to bleed and they could not stop the bleeding. So her instructor called me at home and said that I needed to come and pick her up at the college and take her to the hospital.

I got to the college and she was waiting for me, and I remember she was wearing her white uniform and it had blood stains running down the front of her dress. She had her head tilted back so the blood was running down her throat and into her stomach. She got into the car and I drove her to the hospital. We entered the emergency room and we went up to the receptionist desk and I told them that she has a nose bleed that will not stop and the blood is running in to her stomach, with her head tilted back. They said, *"Take a seat and we will be with you as soon as we can."* I do not believe they thought it was very serious.

We sat for what felt about an hour and I had to go up to the counter again and said, *"Look, she is starting to get sick form all of the blood in her stomach."*

So finally they took her into the emergency room and she sat on the bed and all of a sudden she started vomiting blood all over the nurse and the doctor, the nurse and doctor look like they had seen a ghost they could not believe the amount of blood spuming from her mouth. They actually were in a panic mode trying to figure out how to stop the bleeding. Debbie had told the doctor that she had recently had surgery to correct a nasal passage. The doctor inserted a Catheter up her nose and inflated it to apply pressure in hoping to stop the bleeding. "Thank God" that worked! She was admitted to the hospital, she had lost so much bleed she need a transfusion of blood.

What had happen is one of the arteries that was cauterized in her nose had open up and she was bleeding continuously from this open artery. She needed to have surgery again so they could correct the damage.

I remember going home that night after they admitted her and I was in the garage washing her cloths from all of the blood, I remember it as clear as it was yesterday. My heart was hurting thinking what I would do if I ever lost Debbie. I was so upset I stood by the washing machine and began to cry. This was such a dramatic situation I could not get over.

The next day when I went to work in the morning, I could not stay; I felt I needed to be by Debbie's side. I left work and went to the hospital. She still had the Cather inserted up her nose and was waiting for the doctors to review the x-ray to plan out the operation.

She need more blood so I went down to donate blood for Debbie, I also persuaded guys from work to come and give blood, even if they were not her type at least they were donating blood in her honor.

The surgery was performed and all went well, she was released a few days later, they just wanted to make sure that the operation was a success. After all the healing, we were back on track again.

Debbie had finished her college and received a degree in medical assisting and wanted to pursue her career further by becoming an instructor at the college working with Miss Regan

For her to do this she needed to show the college that she had a high school diploma. That was going to be a problem. You see, we were married at an early age and Debbie quit school in the eighth grade. So for her to do this she need to the GED so she could continue here goal. Of course this was no major task for her to accomplish. She studied and took the test and received her GED like it was no big deal, I always admired her will and confidence, and she always amazed me.

Debbie started working as an aid for the medical assisting program working with Miss Regan, just like she wanted to.

Debbie also joined a softball team and this is when she met Margie White, they became very close friends. Margie had a brother that needed a job and asked if Debbie could see if I could hire her brother Frank. I told Debbie to have him come and see me and I will see what I could do.

Needless to say I hired Frank Muro; I thought he was a very nice and trustworthy person. And we got along very well.

The year was 1988 when we decided move from Norwalk.

We were always thinking about the upbringing of our two sons and felt that the Norwalk area was getting a bit too rough. I was not getting along with my boss very well and thought about changing jobs, but not profession. There was a company in Riverside California that I wanted to look into working there.

Debbie and I one day went up to Running Springs in the San Bernardino Mountains, I'm not sure why we really went up to the mountains. I believe it was for the wedding of Lori and Bob Beck.

It was so nice and peaceful with all of the pine trees and the smell of the open wilderness. So we thought what a perfect place to finish raising the boys. This would be a long commute for me to work in Buena Park, about eighty-three miles one way. I still was in the process of looking for a new job, hoping for something closer to the base of the mountains. We began looking for a house in the Running Springs area or Arrowbear, the connecting town. We search for quite a while before we came across this tri-level house on Arrowbear Dr. We fell in love with this place and decided to move from Norwalk to Arrowbear, the boys were very excited as so was we. We knew that this move was going to be done in a single trip because of the distance, eighty-three miles one way. I persuaded a few guys from work and I borrowed the company stake bed truck and along with some other friends with pickup trucks and a trailer, we packed our entire household goods and made the move.

This house we bought was very unique. The parking was on top of the road and you would walk down a stairway to the front door, you could not see the house from the road. This place was very nice on the inside but needed a lot of work on the outside. It needed handrails up by the parking area; it was about a seven or eight foot drop from the parking area to the front door. The deck was not finished and the stairway was unstable. The retaining wall was made of plywood, just not very pretty to look at.

After we moved in, I started working on a new deck, a new stairway, and building a new retaining wall in my spare time.

Debbie got a job at Lake Arrowhead medical center; this area was full of Hollywood stars. One day she came home to tell me that she meant Priscilla Presley (Elvis's) ex-wife at the medical center, and she was very nice to her, she also met Kevin Costner. One afternoon she and the boys were at the pizza house in Running Springs and in come Ernie Hudson from "Ghost Busters" and got his autograph for the boys and then he came into the medical clinic in Lake Arrowhead with his kids. And he said to her "*Debbie,*" in a joking matter, "*are you following me around or what?*" And one day Debbie and I were standing in line at the post office and guess who came in? Ernie Hudson! He said, "*I just can't get away from you can I.*" She said "*I guess not, this is my husband, Dale.*"

We enjoyed living up in the mountains and of course I was unable to find a job close to the mountains, so I continued to make the long drive to Cerritos. My friend Jack and Bobbie lived in Redondo Beach, so twice a week I would spend the night at their house to break up the long drive home, which I really did not like very much because I would rather be with my family, but the drive was killing me and Debbie and the boys loved it in the mountains and so did I when I was there.
I remember at Christmas we would go caroling with the neighbors, the snow was so beautiful and life was good to us.

Debbie would go down to Palm Springs to warm up; it was only about an hour form where we lived so you could go from the snow to the desert in a short drive. You could have the best of both worlds. No matter how long Debbie and I were apart, we were so connected and so much in love with each other we knew that our souls were always together. We had our moments of disagreements but still we always talk it out, our love for each other was forever.

I remember one summer we decided to go to Maui on vacation with Dee and Danny and there two boys, they were Josh and Dylan's age, they also friends with them.

We went to Maui and had a blast. We stayed at the Hyatt, I believe that was the one it was, it had a swim up bar and waterfall. We rented a mustang convertible (red) did the "Road to Hana." Also we did a submarine ride of the coast of Maui, this sub held about forty people. The trip was so enjoyable, Debbie and I was having the time of our life.

I do remember one Halloween night 1994 we were with Dee and Danny and Lori and Bob and we were going around for trick or treating with the kids and we just left Arrowbear liquor and were heading over to Hoffman elementary school. We pulled out of the liquor store first and drove to the school and Dee and Danny were behind us. This school was only about a mile down the road and as Debbie and I were talking on our way, we pulled into the school parking lot and were waiting for Dee and Danny to be behind us. We parked and waited and I said to Debbie, *"Where are they?"* We sat for a few minutes and I decided to back track to find them. As we pulled out on to the highway and headed around one of the hair pin turns we saw something unexpectedly, a pickup truck on its top and what I thought was a compress white jeep against the side of the mountain side. We stopped and I got out of our Jeep and Lori was screaming to me to get them out of the Jeep. I ran over to the Jeep and Dee was bleeding a lot from her face and she was pinned under the steering wheel and her legs were crushed and Danny was on the floor board.

We spent hours with the EMT's cutting the top off of the Jeep to get them out. Debbie took the kids over to Lori's house so they did not witness the pain and agony that was going on, and Lori went with them. Lori was an emotional a train wreck. I remember the EMT telling me to keep talking to them so they would stay alert; they were fading in and out. It took over an hour to cut them out of the Jeep and took them down to San Bernardino hospital. I was standing there in shock thinking that the truck that hit them head on just missed our Jeep and hit them. I started walking home about a mile in the dark because in the mountains there are no street lights. After I got home I sat down on the couch and I was shaking so bad thinking how something could happen like this and was thanking God it was not Debbie and the boys and me that was hit. I called Debbie at Lori's and told her that I was home and please come home, I was in tears. What an awful ordeal this was.

After the accident we did everything we could for Dee and Danny, we stayed at the hospital many evenings comforting them, helping raise money for them, drove them everywhere they needed to go. We felt so sorry for them. Dee shattered both legs, broke both wrists, she had pins put in her legs and her wrist. Danny broke his back and damaged his legs, and little Danny broke both arms.

I was soon finding out the highway 303 from the base of the mountain to running springs was considered one of the most deadly highways in California. I assisted in two other head on collisions coming home from work where one man died. Debbie and I had a couple almost head on accidents. Luckily our quick thinking and fast reflexes, we avoided them. Joshua was sixteen and was at the age of driving and we certainly did not feel very comfortable about him driving while we lived in the mountains, and I was getting very tired of the commute. My boss was let go at work and I was put into his place and I felt this was my big chance to prove myself to the owner that I was capable of handling this position, as plant manager for CFI.

So we decided that maybe it was time to move down the mountain. We asked the boys where they wanted to live if we moved from the mountains. They both said the "BEACH."

So as good parents would do, we started looking for a house in Huntington Beach. We wanted to get as close to the ocean as possible, but as you know, as close as you get to the ocean the prices are extremely expensive.

We did find a house to rent in Huntington Beach on Ross Lane, maybe about six miles from the water, not too bad.

Now it was time to start packing things up in the mountains for the move. We had the house up for sale but at this time, the houses in the mountains were not moving very well on the market. These were mainly vacation homes, not really for people that worked in the flatlands.

We moved anyway and hoped the house would eventually sell.

Once we were settled in our house that we rented, it sure was nice driving to work instead of three or four hours one way, it was just thirty minutes.

Once the boys were enrolled into school, Debbie was itching to go be to work, she always needed something to keep her mind and her body going. She always wanted to contribute to the household, "God bless her."

She got a job working with a medical group on Beach Boulevard, in Huntington Beach. I remember her coming home and was telling me that she was in one of the doctor's offices, and he said to Debbie, "*I have been in this office for a long time, and every morning I look out my window and I see this view of the graveyard below and reminds me of mistakes that can happen if we do not do our job with pride and expertise, we will be responsible in filling this graveyard.*" That always stuck in my mind and I know in her mind as well.

Our life was moving forward, Debbie and I had our moments but still very much in love with each other. We always came to an understanding one way or another.

One of the most terrible moments I experienced was one morning I was driving to work in my little Nissan pickup truck, now remember we just moved down from the mountains and I had all types of survival accessories in my truck, it was about 5:00 in the morning and I was driving to work on Beach Blvd, in the distance I could see what I thought was a trash can on fire, but as I got closer I notice another little fire behind it. As I got closer and closer the fire seemed to be moving. My eyes got locked on this movement of fire on the right side of the road. As I got within a half a block, I noticed this is someone engulfed in flames, running down the street next to a gas station on the corner of Hazard Street and Beach Blvd. The first thing I thought was that they were filming a movie until it dawned on me "this is for real." I slammed on my breaks, jump out of my truck and grab my fire extinguisher and started running to this person, sparing them as another man stopped and tackled this person to the ground as I continued spraying this person until the fire was out. As I looked over at the gas station, I saw the attendant running down the street as the pump was on fire. Without thinking, I ran over to the pump and sprayed the pump until the fire was out.

I walked over to the man lying down next to the curb in the street with the street light shining down on him. I could not determine what this man looked like he was so badly burned over his entire body; his skin

48

was chard and not a stitch of clothing was visible. He just kept staring at me and saying *"call my mom"*, *"call my mom"*, *"call my mom."* Just then I saw a highway patrol car driving up the street. The officer took over and looked again and grabbed his microphone and started calling in and he flipped a U-turn to block the street. He proceeded to oversee what was going on. I told the officer that this man was on fire and I put him out with my fire extinguisher and also the pump at this station was on fire, I was confused that I did not see a car in the station. I could not figure out what just took place. I gave my statement and I just needed to leave, this was too much for me to look at.

As I got back into my truck, I looked into my review mirror and I could see this man in the street and smoke was still rising from his body with the street light shining through the still dark skies.
I got to work and I called Debbie and I told her of my horrible experience, she said *"Dale why don't you come home. You seem to be too upset to be at work."*

I said *"No, I need to get things done here."* This stayed on my mind until lunch. I could no longer accept this situation without knowing what really happened. I got into my truck and drove to the gas station. I walked up to the gas station attendant and said, *"I was driving by here this morning and I actually helped the person that put the person that was on fire out with my extinguisher, what happen?"* The attendant proceeded to explain that this man walked up to the gas station to purchase a gallon of gas and a Bic lighter. He walked over to the pump and filled up his gallon can, laid the pump down poured the gas over his head said a prayer and flick his Bic lighter to set himself on fire.
I read in the paper the following day this man died from his burns. I thought what a painful way to die.
I was thinking why I am experiencing these things: accident in the mountains, this is GOD preparing me for something, trying to make me a stronger person. I was thinking I hope this is the worst thing I will ever need to experience!

I was at Connie and Rick's house one day, they both worked at Certified Fabricators and they became good friends of ours. I remember one day a friend of theirs drove up with this white mustang car in pretty bad condition, mostly wear due to the age of the car. This guy wanted to sell this mustang. I started thinking Debbie always wanted an old mustang, so I asked him what year is his car, he said 1964 ½, there was only a few hundred that were released before 1965, which was the official release of the Mustang car.

Well this caught my attention. I asked, "*How much do you want for your car?*" I believe he wanted $1,500.00 but the only problem was, it had a standard four speed transmission. Debbie could not drive a stick; she drove with both feet with an automatic transmission.

So I said let me speak with Debbie and see if she might be interested in this being a stick.

Debbie was excited, but a little worried about learning to drive standard transmission. We bought the car, it had a 289 bored out to a 302 holey four barrel carbonators and dual glass packs.

I bought the car and drove it home and I see the beauty that if this car is restored, how awesome this car could look.

So I drove it back and forth to work for a while and in the mean time I was teaching Debbie, or trying to teach her to drive a stick shift and this was not working very well, especially when we were pulling into the driveway and she just about ran into the side of the garage.

So to make things easier for Debbie I started looking for a mechanic that would replace this standard transmission with an automatic. I found this mechanic that specialized in mustang restorations and he located an automatic from a 1965 mustang and had it shipped to California. He rebuilt it for me and installed it in Debbie's car.

This mustang, I wanted to restore it back to the original color which was teal.

I had this problem; I was working so hard to bring this car back to life. Debbie was always saying this is your car not mine, but I was fixing it up for her. I guess I started getting a little bit more attached to it.

I re-did the front and back seats, put in new carpet, and had the windows tinted. Also, I was a bit over controlling when it came to this car. Debbie got to the point that she just did not want to drive it after a while. She was afraid something would go wrong when she would be driving and she would feel guilty, so she really stopped driving it all together.

During this time we felt we needed to buy our own home, which we could not afford in California without a large down payment or already own one. We had neither, so Debbie being the person she was, would do whatever she could to make our family happy. She started looking i to manufactured homes, and a trailer park that she felt comfortable in.

I remember her taking me on Beach Blvd. in Westminster looking at homes. We visited quite a few sales lots until she saw the one that captured her eye. Instantly she fell in love with this style of home.
She worked her magic with the sales person, she is a tough nut when it comes to purchasing anything, and she is going to get the most out of our money.

She found a trailer park on Talbert Avenue in Fountain Valley. She liked a lot. The managers, Jack and Liana, very friendly and they were a bit older than us. Debbie thought they would be good managers and there was not a lot of kids around, which made it quiet and comfortable.
I remember one day Debbie and I went over to the park and Debbie showed me this empty lot and said, "Here is where our new home is going to be." She was so excited I still can feel the adrenalin from that moment.

I remember the day they brought our home to the lot. I was at work and Debbie was right there instructing the guys how she wanted her home to be set up. She was walking on a cloud, that's how I always wanted to her to be, "walking on clouds."

She got very busy packing up the house, directing me and the boys on what needed to be done. My work at this time was so demanding it was hard for me to try to arrange the move so Debbie did as much as she could, but the heavy things she needed help with. So one evening I needed to do the move after work and I thought I had enough people to help, but only one or two guys showed up. It made it hard to get it done in one evening, lucky this new home was only about four or five miles away from where we were on Ross Lane in Huntington Beach.

After we settled in, Debbie and I wanted to plan another vacation. Every year we went somewhere and we always made the boys go with us. We were planning another trip to Maui and also Kowhai this time just the four of us, no other friends on this trip. We were tired of all the drama of past friends that had hang-ups. Debbie was getting close to turning forty and she said, *"I'm almost forty and I'm going to make a list of who are my true friends and who are not."* And of course, quite of few did not make Debbie's list.

We went to Maui and we had a blast, it was just so nice with just us. We went at our own pace and did what we wanted to do without someone else wanting to change our plans to satisfy them. We canoed down the river where *Indiana Jones* was filmed, only a third of the island you're able to travel by car; we had a great relaxing family vacation.

Once we returned from vacation, things were going up and down at work. Our company was going up for sale and this was sending an uncomfortable vibe through our lives.

Certified Fabricators was sold, I believe it was 1998, and come the fall of 2000 I was let go from the company after seventeen years of service. It was a major blow to me and Debbie. I really did not see this coming, I must have been looking the other way. It smacked me right upside the head.

I called Debbie and I told her that I was being let go at the end of the month and she was very upset. She asked, *"What are we going to do?"* I said, *"Give me a bit and I will clean out my office, I will be home."* I got home and the next day I called up my longtime friend from Boeing and I told him I was looking for work. He said, *"What you out of a job? Are you willing to move?"* I said let me talk to Debbie. He said he would call me later. I talked to Debbie and she was willing to move. Dylan was graduating in a few months and really nothing was keeping us here. Debbie said that she was ready for another adventure. Also my cousin, Frank, had a farm in Maui and was looking for someone within the family to help him run it. We spoke a few times on the phone trying to decide if that would work for us but Debbie did not want to go too far from the families and she was right.

So the next day I got a call from my friend from Boeing and he asked, "Would you be willing to move to Michigan to a company called Odyssey?" I remember a few years before I was sent out to Odyssey by Boeing to help them for a couple of weeks on some bond tools.

I said hold on a minute, and I said, *"Debbie you want to move to Michigan?"* She shook her head *"Yes."* Randy said, *"They are expecting a call from you."*

So after I got off the phone, she already had the map out looking where Michigan was and pointed right there it is on the map to where it was on the map.

So Debbie said *"let's do it."* With a big grin, I said I would call Jeff; he was the VP of Odyssey. We talked on the phone and we agreed on a wage. He said, *"We will fly you and your wife out here next weekend and we can talk."* Debbie and I went to Detroit and we stayed at the Winsor casino, in Winsor Canada.

I did the interview with Jeff and things could not have gone any better. I had a new job while I was still on payroll with Certified Fabricators.

After returning from this trip, Debbie was excited about another "new" adventure. We were getting a bit tired of California living and too much traffic.

We started packing our things up. Debbie got a hold of a realtor and was putting our house up for sale. We knew that it would not take too long to sell the house. Debbie had done so much, she decorated the house. It looked very nice and we lived in a good area of Fountain Valley. We scheduled the movers to pick up our furniture and our things were to be placed in storage until we found a place to live. The day of Dylan's graduation, Debbie and I picked up the car and right after Dylan's party we left for Michigan. I remember it was around morning, we started our drive heading east. We took our time stopping at Jack and Bobbie's house on the way; they lived in Colorado, outside of Denver, for a couple of days to visit. We enjoyed the drive. Debbie and I always loved road trips. I remember Dylan was unsure of this new adventure, he was not too happy about leaving his friends.

Once we got to Michigan, we had arranged to stay at this extended stay hotel not too far from where I was working. We spent quite a while there while we contacted a realtor. I remember at work I was trying to fit in, remember I worked as a Certified Fabricators for seventeen years so there was going to be some getting used to the new surroundings.

Debbie had to leave for California to close on our house so she decided to leave it up to me and Dylan to find a house with the realtor. So Dylan and I were trying to find a place between Odyssey and Global Tooling, these were the two sister companies I was going to work for.

We looked at a lot of houses and we saw this one in Washington Township that felt good to us. Dylan and I both agreed on this is house being the one. I called Debbie and said we found a house to buy. This house was yellow color and it was moved there for a gravel pit some miles away. It looked like it was built in the early 1920's, not sure because there was no record of the actual age of this house. We put an offer on the house and when Debbie came back we took her over to see the house and I think she was fine with it. I knew she was tired and wanted to have our own home. Washington Township was founded in 1827. This was an old area and in talking to some of the people that this area was populated by Indians many moons ago.

This house had a front porch that extended the full length of the house. It had two front doors: one off the living room and one off the den that was added on after the house was moved there in the sixties from a gravel pit off of 26 Mile Road a few miles away. As you enter the house to the left is the den, off the den is a two car garage, to the left was the kitchen, and if you walk straight, there were stairs that led down to the basement. Entering the kitchen and the dining room, all of the wood work was this thick molding around the doorways and windows. There was a reading bench under the window with drawers under for storage. To the left was the entry hall, to the left was the bathroom, and to the right across from that was the master bed room. Back through the dining room, you enter the living room with the original front door with a full length beveled glass window; the door lock had the old skeleton key hole. At the opposite side of the room, a coat closet and the stairway leading up the second floor all made of very old looking wood. Once you started upstairs halfway up is this small platform that made a ninety degree turn, then you proceed to the second floor. At the top to the left was one of the bedrooms with another window bench recess in the wall. As you turn right and start down the hall there is another bedroom to your left and a bathroom to your right, and straight was a small closet, on the right you enter the last bedroom at the end of the hallway. At the far end of this bedroom was a door that you could step out onto the top of the den below. We could not find any records of the history of this house. The only thing we could find was that the deed said the house was built in the forties. Once Debbie returned from California, I told her that we found the perfect house. After about a month had past, one afternoon Debbie and Dylan had returned from the store and Debbie went to the bathroom. She heard the sound of water running, it sound like it was coming from the basement floor. Debbie and Dylan proceeded to the basement to find out where the water sound was coming from. They saw water running from behind boxes stacked up against the wall. Debbie and Dylan thought a water line must of burst. They began to remove the boxes from the wall where the water was coming from, and behind the boxes they saw a faucet opened that the water was pouring out of. They turned the faucet off and it was hard to turn off. They could not figure out why this faucet was turned on. They could not figure out how this got turned on, this was very odd. I remember Debbie called me up at work and we both were puzzled at this event happening.

One day Debbie and I were upstairs in the middle bedroom, thinking how we were going to arrange this bedroom. In the corner of this room we placed an old rocking chair. So we were talking about the decoration, this chair started moving back and forth, slowly as if someone or something was moving this chair. We were a little spooked, at least I was very uncomfortable with this happing, and I felt very uneasy.

I remember one evening Debbie and I had returned home from visiting the neighbors across the street and when I unlocked and opened the front door, we both smelled a strong fragrance of lavender perfume, this fragrance lingered in one spot as we entered the house, we thought another odd encounter.

I recall around the middle of June 2001, we planned on going to Florida to meet Jack and Bobbie along with their two girls, Lisa and

Jessica for the weekend at Universal Studios. We had a wonderful weekend but of course the time flew by.

We returned home late Sunday evening and of course I needed to go to work in the morning. I had a hard time getting comfortable in bed, I kept tossing and turning until Debbie said, *"Dale, go to the couch to sleep. You are keeping we awake."*

So I grabbed my pillow and proceeded to get comfortable on the couch in the den.

I was awakened by the sound of someone running down the stairs. I could hear Dylan saying, *"Dad there's a bat in my bedroom!"*

I said Dylan, *"Just get rid of it, just open your window and shoo it out."* He said, *"No you get out."* I could hear Debbie saying, *"What is going on out there?"* Dylan said, "Mom there's a bat in my bedroom!"

So I got up and said, *"Ok l,et's get prepared for this."* and first thing that came to mind was the movie the "Great Outdoors" with Dan Aykroyd and John Candy. I grab a broom, cloth basket for my face and gloves. I proceed upstairs with Dylan in tow, walking down the hallway looking for this bat. Once I enter Dylan's bedroom he grabbed the doorknob and closed the door behind me. I said Dylan, *"Open this door!"* He said, *"Not until you get the bat out of my room!"*

This bat put up quite a bit of a battle. I would knock to the floor with the broom, the bat would start biting the on the broom, I kept smacking it and once it was biting the broom I slung it out the door. It flew out and turned around and flew right back into the bedroom and the battle continued on.

Finally I was able to sling out with the broom again and got the door shut, this battle must have lasted about thirty minutes and Dylan's bedroom looked like a tornado just came through.

One day after work, as I entered the house, I noticed that all of the lights were on in the den, kitchen, and living room. I thought this was odd. I went up stairs and the lights were on up there as well. So I came back down the stairs and was looking around. Debbie and Dylan were gone, not sure where. So I proceeded looking around and on the kitchen counter was a business card from the Macomb County sheriff's office, and on the side of the card it read: *We received a 911 hang up call from your house and we entered through the side door, and there were no of signs of disturbance, so we left.*

So once Debbie arrived home, I told her the odd story and showed her this card. She said, *"That was strange, maybe somehow the telephone lines got crossed and someone really needed help."*
She called the sheriff's office and explained what happened, and the lady dispatcher at the sheriff's office said *"That is not possible; let me explain how 911 calls work. We can trace it to the exact line in your house and this came from within your house and this call came from within your house."*

We were puzzled no one was home and we did not do it. Then we thought maybe some kid came in and did it as a joke, we did not know be we were sure after that to make sure all our doors were locked when we left the house from that day forward

Now the odd thing seemed to be happening more often. Often when Debbie would come home she would announce that she was home if he was not down in the living room. Well one afternoon Dylan was upstairs and he heard the front door open and shut and he heard Debbie's voice "Dylan I'm home." He waited for a while and he did not hear his mom any more so he went down stairs and said *"MOM?"* he called out to her a few times then he looked outside and did not see her car, she was still gone, this is still an unexplained incident.

It wasn't long after we moved in that at night we could hear creaking of the wooden floors and they sounded like footsteps walking back and forth, from one end of the hall to the other which stretch the full length of the house. After a few months, the walking footsteps started becoming more frequent and clearer sounding that these were footsteps of someone walking. Dylan said that he could hear the walking sounds coming up to his bed in the middle of the night and turn around and walk away. One night Dylan was woken up by the footsteps coming up to his bed and then he felt someone or something sit on the end of his bed, he jumped up and ran down the stairs and woke Debbie and I up saying, *"Someone sat on my bed"*, he was a bit shaken up about that.

I remember Debbie had a Bunko group she started with her bowling friends, Judy Middleton, Brigit and some other women.

Once a month they would meet at a different player's house. One night Debbie was going out for Bunko and Dylan said, *"Dad I'm going out tonight."* I told him, *"No, you need to stay here with me."* He said *"No, I got to go."*

I never felt very comfortable staying at home by myself; I was a bit freaked out about this situation with the unknowns in this house. I would not go up stairs at all if I was alone. And I did not like staying home alone, especially at night. I remember that night I was watching TV for awhile and then went to bed. As I was watching TV in bed I started hearing the footsteps walking from the far end of the house upstairs, walking over to the bedroom where I was laying and walking to the other far end of the house and back again and again. This was freaking me out and I could not wait until Debbie got home, I felt better when she got home, what a relief.

Another odd situation we encountered that took place was this little Uncle Sam holding an American flag. Debbie had it as a nick- knack on top of the television; she noticed that when she would be dusting, Uncle Sam would be moved to the entertainment center. One day she said, "Who keeps moving this Uncle Sam?"

Dylan and I said, *"Neither one of has been moving this Uncle Sam."* She said, *"This kept moving over to the entertainment center and if I want it there I will put it over there."*

We were puzzled Dylan and I, and just disregarded this issue.

So one afternoon Dylan was in the kitchen by the sink and out of the corner of his eye he saw and object go flying across the living room. He went into the living room and saw this little Uncle Sam lying on the couch with its American flag broken off.

One afternoon we were out talking with our neighbors and asked if anyone that lived there before had said anything about weird things happening in the house. Of course they looked at us like we were crazy!

So another night, about three in the morning, the door bell started ringing and we got up to answer the door and it was the sheriff's again. The officer said, *"Is everything fine? We received a 911 call from this house and we are here to investigate it."*

So we let the officers in but we did not say anything about the previous 911 call, we just told them we do not know how this was called in, we were all sleeping. He searched the house and then left. We went back to sleep.

Another incident was when my son and Heidi came to visit us for a week.

In the mean time I was struggling with my new job here. I just was having a hard time adjusting to the new environment and surroundings. Debbie also was having a hard time here too. We noticed that most of the people we encountered were not too friendly. It's like they would have their small circle of family and friends and you did not venture into their space. So Debbie and I were pretty much stuck to ourselves. I do remember Debbie wanted to join a bowling league. So she went over to Romeo Bowling Alley and signed up for a league. That is when she met Judy, they became very good friends; this was also the beginning of her friendship with Brigit and Marilyn, and a number of girls. Debbie was very happy with this group of ladies she became friends with. So now Debbie wanted to start up a Bunko group. Judy asked Debbie "Where are you going to get twelve ladies to come every week for a Bunko group?" And Debbie said, *"We will find them."* They came, (even twelve years later the same group of ladies still meet every week for Bunko).

In the meantime, since we were so close to Canada we could be there in just a forty-five minute drive. We started going to the casino in Sarnia to Point Edwards. We would go just to get away for Sunday afternoons and it was a gorgeous drive. We would do pretty well. I remember one time I was playing the quarter slots and hit something like $1900.00, so while I was waiting to be paid I was playing the machine right next to it and hit for $1500.00. Debbie could not believe that happened. We collected our monies and went home happy.

Also Karen and Gary Laible were living back in Niagara Falls, NY and it was only about a five hour drive from our house going through Canada. So we gave them a call and we started rekindling our friendship. We were very close in the mid-seventies until the move back to New York and we lost contact for many years.

I remember going to their house on our first visit in many, many years and Debbie and Karen connected like they never miss a beat. We made many trips to their house during the time we were still living in Michigan. Debbie and Karen would hang out and Gary and I would go metal detecting for musk balls and coins and whatever else we would find.

Debbie and I were still not happy in Michigan and wanted to go home to California, we just did not fit there. So we decided to move back to California and we put up our house for sale, but we kept it very quiet, I did not want my work finding out what we were planning.

Once we found a buyer for our house we started having garage sales and giving things away, we wanted to make this move light, but still keeping our cherished possessions.

Debbie was such a great planner, she had everything packed up and had a moving company come and load everything; they were going to store the trailer in their yard until we got to California and then they would deliver our things to a storage unit for us until we found a house to move into, she was wonderful at organizing these events since we moved so much in the past.

I remember the day we left Michigan. We were in our Ford Windstar van and driving down the road to the border of Ohio, we felt so relieved and free and extremely happy. We had not felt like this in years!
Where were we going, we were just not sure, but we were leaving Michigan going west somewhere.

We decided to stop at French Lick Resort; we had been there with my dad and stepmom a couple of times before and were taken in by this resort and the west Badin that was just up the road. This resort was under restoration very beautiful built around the early twenties. I do believe Roy Clark was an entertainer playing that night, we were able to attend the show, and it was a very good performance.

The next day we went over to the riding stable that was next to the reproduction home that was modeled after Thomas Jefferson's home. This home was built by the son of the gentlemen who built French Lick Resort in the 1800's. A weird story is connected to this home. The wife of the son, she hung herself from the stairway in the late 1800's or early 1900's. She was not fond of the resort and I think she was a bit crazy; they had a daughter I believe died there as well.

Also the owner's horse was buried in the front with a head stone; I forgot what the horse's name was. The house also had a circle driveway in front; you could tell no one had lived there for many years While we were talking to the lady that owned the riding stables we were asking her about the Thomas Jefferson home over on the hill. She was not bashful at all. She had said that some time in the evening she would see this little girl about six or seven years old, coming down from the hill to see the horses. She asked the little girl where she lived and she told her, the house on the hill. No one lived in the house for thirty or forty years. We thought that was bizarre, apparently this was a, spirit!

We were travelling with Toto our dog so we needed to keep her as quiet as possible while we were out, and she seemed to be fine staying in the room to sleep.

We began on our journey the next day heading on to Arizona. We drove to Phoenix and stayed at a motel and were contemplating on if we want to try to stay there for a while. Debbie and I were just so glad to be in the west again. I looked through the local paper for steel companies and we drove around the city to get a feel for things. We drove down to Tucson, there was a fabrication company I was interested in checking out, but the area was not quite up to par. Then we decided to continue our journey to California.

Once we made it to California, we were looking for a place to stay in the Buena Park area. A motel, hotel whatever, we did not even have a place to stay in California, that's how Debbie and I pretty much rolled; care free, and it felt good.

So we found a hotel right on Beach Blvd. by the Wax Museum, and Medieval Times that would allow pets because we had Toto, the mini-pincher?.

I spoke with Stuart Gordon on the phone a few times while we were living in Michigan. I told him that when we first started thinking about moving back to California. He was the president of Votaw Precision Technologies another aircraft tooling company. He said if I was interested in moving back to California to give him a call, he would set up with a job.

So once we got settled into our hotel room, I gave Gordon a call and asked if the job offer was still good. He said go by and "let's" talk.

The next morning I drove over to Santa Fe Springs, only about ten miles from where we were staying.

I interviewed with Gordon and was hired on the spot. I called Debbie and she was so relieved and happy. I loved seeing that smile on her face, they were so warming to me and I melted in her presence, and even today I can still see her smile embedded in my mind!

Now we needed to find a house to rent, and trust me rentals are hard to come by in the area without costing an arm and a leg. And of course in California you needed to fill out an application and get approved to rent; not saying we were worried about it, we were not. Our credit was above average, almost as good as you could get. That was one thing about Debbie; she was always on top of our bills, never missing a due date.

It was hard to find a place that would rent to us because of Toto the dog, not many places allowed dogs unless they were dumps. At times I said we may need to get rid of the dog. Debbie would not do that at all. *"Toto is part of the family we will just keep looking."* she would say.

Most of the places we found, by the time we called they were already rented. Debbie drove by this house and it was empty and they were working on it, so she stopped and asked if this house was going to be for rent? They said after they put in new carpet and fix the bathroom up a bit. So Debbie, with her warm personality, spoke to the lady and explained we just moved from Michigan and was looking for a house to rent.

The landlord told Debbie they do not allow pets. Debbie said we have a little min-pin and will pay extra to keep the dog, I believe she added $ 25.00 or $50.00 more a month, and so we could have Toto with us.

This house was not quite what I was wanting, it was built in the fifties and it had seen better days and it made me feel like I was taking steps back in life instead of progressing. Of course Debbie did not feel that way at all, she was always happy as long as we were a family and had money to pay bills and eat. Of course more is better, but it did not matter to her as much as it did for me, I always wanted to perform my best as a provider.

Our back yard had a brick block wall surrounding the back yard with a wooden gate. I remember one day Dylan had mowed the back yard and forgot to close the gate, apparently Toto got out. Debbie called me on the phone extremely upset saying, *"Toto got of the yard and I don't see her anywhere."* Now picture this, we lived off a residential street. At one end was a school and the other end ran out to a six lane highway, very busy and no idea which direction this could have lead her too. I said, *"Debbie, I don't know what to say she is most likely gone now."*

Well Debbie will not accept that answer. Debbie decided she would go door to door down our entire street. At the end of this street was a school, so she figured if nobody had seen Toto she would search the school. As Debbie knocked on the last door before entering the school, this lady answered the door and Debbie asked if she had seen a little brown and black min-pin. The lady said, *"As a matter fact we were driving on Knott Blvd and this little dog was following a kid on a bicycle and went cross the busy street. This dog sat on the sidewalk, so we know this dog was lost and so we pick up this dog and brought it home. We were get ready to make up some flyer to post around for a lost dog."* This was so odd that these people lived on our street and found Toto on the main street, if they did not rescue Toto she would not be with me still today.

Debbie was so happy and relieved at the same time, what determination my Debbie has.

About six months had passed and we are doing pretty well. Debbie wanted to start square dancing and I was not to keen on the idea, but she had wanted to do this for a long time, so I gave in and said ok. Of course she went right to work finding a park and recreational in Buena Park right down the road from us that had square dancing classes. Of course I had no excuse not to go, so we joined and going with Debbie was always fun no matter what it was, she made it enjoyable for me. She always wanted to please me, and she did very well at that. After a few lessons we were getting pretty good or at least we thought we were; we kept to ourselves a lot.

By this time my work was going up for sale. I thought not again! This is going to drive me nuts; I just wanted to be a bit more settled in one spot for a while. The old owner of Votaw bought the place back got rid of my boss and appointed the new VP and president, and of course we were not on the same page a lot of times.

I have a vacation coming up so Debbie and I decided to go to Houston, Texas to visit her aunt and maybe look for a new job. I was always looking if I felt uncomfortable and I felt that at Votaw now.
I found a few possibilities but nothing I could count on, and time was running out on vacation so I decided to go back to work and Debbie was going to stay another week. Well once I returned from vacation I was only at work a couple of days and I received a pink slip. I was being laid off!

I called up Debbie in Texas and said, *"Debbie I just got laid off of work and I'm packing up my things and going home."* She was shocked to say the least; she said she would leave to come home tomorrow.

After she came home, she was really not to terribly worried, we been through this before. I applied for unemployment and also up dated my resume and posted it on monster.com. In the mean time Debbie got a job working part time as receptionist, answering phones and doing what she could to help make ends meet.

I received a hit on my site from a man in Fayetteville, Arkansas name Joe Madder, who was the owner of an aircraft tooling company and was interested in my experiences in the aircraft field.

I gave Joe a call and he wanted to meet me and tour his campus, sounded great to me and Debbie. I told him that we would be more than happy to come to Arkansas to be interviewed for the position of a manager that was available.

So I went down and had new tires put on our Windstar van and Debbie and I started our journey to Arkansas. We had nothing better to do and it looked like it could be a place we would be willing to move too.

Once we arrived in Fayetteville wc checked in to the motel and decided that a drive over to per see the "CAMPUS", he invited me to see.

When we drove up, all we saw was this tin building and was kind of puzzled thinking, what campus?

So keeping a positive outlook the next morning I arrived at the company to meet Joe, he was a very unusual individual. He kept talking around in circles and he didn't make any sense, he did not say I had the job, but he did not say I didn't, he gave my $300.00 for my time and said he would get back to me in a couple of weeks.

So I went back to the hotel where Debbie was and I told her my experience with Joe, and she said, *"At least we had a road trip that was long overdue."*

We decided to spend a couple of days there and had a good time doing that seeing the sights of Fayetteville.

After arriving back home I continued looking for work, spending time reading at home and doing what I could. I decided to get a hold of a co-worker, Ted Rinker; He worked with me at Certified Fabricators to see if there was any opening at Coast Composites, where he worked.

He said *"I will talk to my boss Colin Britles, and get back with you."* So after a few days Ted called and said that Colin wanted me to come by for an interview. I went over to Coast Composites; it was about thirty-four miles south for Buena Park, where we were living.

I met with Colin Birtles, he was rather nice and I felt very comfortable with him, we went over to the president's office, Jerry Anthony; he was not to bad a little abrasive but still not too bad. After the interview I felt very confident that this was going to work out alright.

The only problem was getting them to make up their minds on when I was to be hired. In the meantime, I received a call from Joe Madder letting me know that he was going to be in San Francisco and wanted me to meet him there for a second interview; I was puzzled about this now.

So Debbie and I talked about it and decided to give it a go. So we gathered up some cloths, packed our bags and Debbie got us a good deal on a hotel close to the bay.

We drove to San Francisco; I believe it took about seven or eight hours to get there. We did not think about it being cool until we got there and the wind was blowing pretty well, and of course we did not bring any sweater or coats. So we ended up buying a couple of sweaters, we seem to have this problem everywhere we go. We end up with sweaters from places like Canada, we just don't think about cool places until we get there.

Well, we meet Joe for dinner and he had brought his fifteen year old daughter to dinner with us. He proceeded to talk about this position at his company but would not make up his mind if I had the job or not. After dinner we knew no more than we did when we sat down for dinner, this man was so unreadable, even still today I'm puzzled.

But Debbie and I still had a wonderful time, going to China Town, riding the street cars, shopping, this was one of Debbie's favorite things to do. After a few days there we decided to drive home and move on to what was for us next.

I remember Colin calling one afternoon, letting me know that I was hired. That was a good feeling, and a relief. I remember going to Coast Composites and meeting with Colin and he was showing me around the shop, nothing that I was surprised to see, same work I've done most of the years. Then he took me over to the program management room. It was so small with four desks and of course one was empty, right next to good old Ted. Now Ted is a very abrasive individual to say the least, but he means well, it's just his approach to people he is a big brut. And of course you are pretty much on your own; do not ask for any help from him.

Now the drive was only about thirty-two miles but in southern California, thirty-two miles could take about two hours at traffic time coming and going on the 405 or the 5 freeways.

After about a few months, we decided to move closer to my work, so Debbie starting looking for a place closer to Coast Composites. She found a condo in Laguna Nigel, close to Irvine where I work at. It was about nine miles which was great!

This condo was 1100 sq ft. and two bedrooms and Dylan was living with us so it was a bit small, but it was better than where we were. Dylan was working for UPS, just starting his career in the logistics field. So I got a couple of friends, Frank Muro and Rick Stevenson, to help us move; we were able to complete this in one weekend thanks to Debbie's well organization skills for moving.

I was slowly getting settled in at Coast Composite. Things were going well, but every now and then I was feeling a bit out of place.

I remember Debbie went to see Joshua and Heidi in Riverside, Wisconsin, where they were living with Heidi's mom and dad, Bill and Mary. They went out to dinner to an Irish restaurant and while they were there, Debbie saw a flyer on the counter by the register, advertising Castledaly Manor in Ireland. This was a guided tour, one price for airfare, bus pick up at Dublin airport to the manor, and daily bud trips to different parts of Ireland.

Once Debbie got home and showed me the information she picked up, we started checking into taking a vacation to Ireland. Debbie was part Irish and one of her dreams was to go to Ireland, and I was also excited about going as well.

So Debbie did a little investigating on what the trip would cost us, and what was the best time to go,
And where were the daily trips going too?

We scheduled our trip for May 19th – May 2seventh of 2004, the cost for this trip was $1,850.00 for two people, what a deal! This included airfare from Chicago to Dublin and eight days at the manor, we still needed to purchase our tickets to and from Chicago. This was so exciting for us, neither one of us had been over to Europe before. This was going to be a wonderful adventure, we could just feel it!

We were shopping, packing and just could not wait for this day to come, and when it did we were as gitty as couple of school kids. Our flight was from Santa Ana (John Wayne airport) to Chicago and then on to Dublin. Once we landed in Chicago we had four of five hours to kill. So Joshua and Heidi met us at the Hilton at the airport for dinner, we had a wonderful time visiting with the kids.

Our flight was leaving Chicago at 7:40 pm; this was on a Thursday, on Air Lingus. This was going to be about a seven hour flight. Debbie made sure that our sets were off the one side, the way the seats ran was two seats on one side, five in the middle and two on the other side. We tried to sleep but were just not comfortable enough to do so. Our plane landed in Dublin around, I believe 8 or 9 am. After de-boarding we went through immigration and walked into a very busy and crowded airport and were told by Harp and Eagle to look for the man holding the sign saying "Castledaly." We must have been in a daze, we walked right by him and did not see him and walked a bit and then back dragging our luggage until we saw him right where we started. After picking up our luggage, we walked up to the driver and told him we were part of this tour and he asks us to stand over with this small group of tourist off to the side. After he felt all of us were together, he came over and introduced himself to us as Peter the driver and Declan the tour guide. We gathered our belonging and headed across the parking lot, as you cross the street of course you always look to your left here in the states, but over there you need to look to the right since they do drive on the other side of the road, this was very strange for us. Once we got on to the bus, Declan said that our first stop was going to be in Athlone, where we could exchange our dollars into Euros, and visit the oldest working pub in Ireland "Sean's Bar" built in 600 AD, open as a pub and still after hundreds of years is still a pub. He also said that they wanted us not to go to sleep, we needed to adjust to the time difference and that's why they were stopping in Athlone and then picking us up at 4:30pm to go to the manor. Of course Debbie and I were struggling to stay awake, I remember Debbie was sitting by the window and her head was nodding back and forth against the window and it startled her and she would wake up.

Once we got to Athlone, the bus dropped us off in front of the main plaza and we were excited to go and visit the oldest pub. Once we entered this pub, we could see the floor was on a slant so when it rained back in the old days the water would wash out all of the spilled debris out the back door. This pub was quite intriguing. Just old things, all around dark and coffined, but a very welcoming environment. I remember this section of the wall was cut away with glass covering it and you could see into the wall and see the old branches and mud that made up the walls from way back then during construction in 600 AD. My first pint of Guinness in Ireland was at Sean's Bar, it was so wonderful to be sitting in a pub in Ireland having a pint or two.

After we were done we went over to the Bank of Ireland to do the currency exchange. We had seen this round castle by the Shannon River, so we decided to take a look around it, and noticed it was called the Adamson Castle built in 1691, this was surprising to us , since Debbie's ancestor were from Ireland. By this time it was time for us to be picked up by the bus to continue on the manor. Castledaly was built in 1760 and it was a private home, quite large with house stable built in the back, they were converted into guest rooms. I believe between the manor and the converted stable it held twenty-two couples. We were lucky to have one of the new converted stable rooms newly build. The manor on the other hand had limited hot water for guests in the morning for showers. Where we were there was no problem with the hot water and we liked being away from the manor a bit, it was quiet in the evening. The manor had its own bar and a lot of locals would come in the evening to meet the Americans and have conversations. So in the evening it got to be a bit noisy.

They served dinner in the main hall of the manor, but the first night after the orientation and what trips are scheduled for the week, Debbie and I went to our room to lay down for a bit, but we fell asleep and when we woke up it was light outside still and we were so confused we thought it was morning, but it was still evening, like 10:00pm. So we went over to the manor to the bar and I ordered a Guinness, I believe Debbie wanted an Irish coffee, and of course Debbie is so friendly and loveable before I even got our drink she was sitting down and was involved in a conversation with some of the people on our tour, laughing and having a grand old time. The tours that you could take daily were €30 euro per person, this was an all day event that went to different parts of southern Ireland. The bus left CastleDaly at 8:30 AM, right after breakfast.

The first day of our trip was to Galway Bay. This is a village right by the Atlantic Ocean; this was a very awesome city. Let me say this, our tour guide Peter and Declan were the most intriguing pair. Peter was a history teacher and a very good singer, his voice was at the top of any Irish singer I have ever heard. Declan was another of the most well informed people of the history of Ireland, it seemed their intelligence was mind blowing. Time on the bus went by so fast listening to these gentlemen that we were in Galway Bay in no time at all. We got off the bus next to the river that emptied into the bay, Peter said, *"We will pick you all up at 4:30 pm and we will head back to the manor."* We got off the bus and did not know what direction to go in, we just start walking and found ourselves in the midst of this gathering of locals singing and playing instruments. One of the songs they sang was... "No" na- never "no" na- never no- more. I remember looking in Debbie's face and she was crying, tears running down her face. Crying of joy she was so taken back by this experience she was in tears. She was walking on clouds that day. We found this interesting place to have lunch with our group. I remember I had Sheppard's pie and not sure what Debbie had but it came with three different types of potatoes. Once was finished, she pushed her plate to the side and Jerry our driver said *"Aren't you going to finish these potatoes?"* Debbie said, *"I'm too full to eat another bit."* Jerry then said, *"Well can I have your potato? We here in Ireland eat all of our potatoes!"*

After doing a bit of shopping we saw this old church built in the eleventh century and I was on a mission to collect rock, pottery, anything old and these were my souvenirs not reproduction of trinkets but something from the actual land of Ireland. So we were walking around this old church by the cemetery and I saw this rock, it looked rather interesting so I dropped it into my pocket. Well it was time to head to the bus,

Once we all were on the bus and heading back to the manor, I was checking out my rock collection and the one I found at the church was actually a human bone. Debbie was not too thrilled about that but I kept it anyway. Once we got back to the manor, Debbie and I wanted to freshen up and take a cab back to Athlone for dinner and she mentioned it to a couple she had been talking to on this trip, and of course they were up to it and then another couple and another. So by the time we were ready to call a cab we need a van to take all of us to Athlone. We went back to Sean's Bar for a few drinks and then we decided to look for a place for dinner. After dinner, off course we headed around town checking out the side streets, it was like being in a different world compared to the States. After walking around a bit, we found ourselves in front for Sean's Bar again had a couple more drinks and called for our cab. The van was not available so we needed two cabs to get all of us back to the manor.

Once we were back, I do believe we called it a day and turned for in for the evening, excited for our next trip in the morning.

The next morning we headed over to the manor for breakfast, which consist of blood sausage, poached eggs and ham. The blood sausage I could not ever try, just the sound of it turned me and Debbie off.

Well it was time for us to hop on the bus and this day we were heading to Dublin City, about two hours from the manor. Of course Jerry and Declan entertained us the entire way. They dropped us off by Trinity College where the Book of Kells is on display; the manuscript contains the four Gospels of the Christian scriptures written in the late sixth through the early ninth centuries, in monasteries in Ireland. Each day at Trinity College they turn the page of the book that is displayed in a glass case. So of course this was something we needed to see so that was our first stop.

After leaving the College I wanted to find the "Hard Rock Café", I wanted a shirt from there. Got the a shirt and headed down the River Liffey. Did a lot of shopping and this is where Debbie and I bought our Claddagh rings, it is a traditional ring given as a token of friendship, love or marriage. The design and customs associated with it originated in the Irish fishing village of Claddagh, located just outside the city of Galway Bay. The ring was first produced in the seventeenth century, though elements of the design date to the late Roman period. Claddagh rings are commonly used as friendship rings, but are most commonly used as engagement/wedding rings. In Ireland, America and other places, the Claddagh is handed down mother-to-daughter or grandmother-to-granddaughter. The way that a Claddagh ring is worn on the hand is usually intended to convey the wearer's relationship status:

1. On the right hand with the point of the heart toward the fingertips, the wearer is single and may be looking for love. (This is most commonly the case when a young woman has first received the ring from a relative, unless she is already engaged).
2. On the right hand with the point of the heart toward the wrist, the wearer is in a relationship, or their heart has been "captured."
3. On the left hand with the point of the heart toward the fingertips, the wearer is engaged.
4. On the left hand with the point of the heart toward the wrist, the wearer is married

We found these gold rings and they were our sizes, it was meant to be for us to buy these and we love them very much. This actually put the icing on the cake, for me.

We had such a wonderful day in Dublin the time just flew by and now it was time to head back to the waiting bus. Tonight we decided to eat at the manor. On the menu was hamburgers, we thought this would be interesting to try, and then we will hang out at the pub in the manor. Once we sat down for dinner we got our food. The burgers were "fabulous", very juicy and great tasting. Debbie had to find her way to the kitchen to discover how these were made. The cook was more than happy to explain how she prepared them. She used ketchup they call "red sauce" and other spices and she bakes them in the oven like meatloaf. We decided to turn in early that night; we were going to have another busy day tomorrow.

The next morning we were heading to Clonmacnoise, a monastery founded in 548 AD. Eight church ruins, two high crosses and two round towers. This is one of Ireland's most important religious sites. Nested along the Shannon River, over the centuries, this site was plundered by the Vikings and all valuables were taken and the home burned to the ground, and the monks rebuilt each time.

We also stopped by the bog lands, this area covered one-fifth of Ireland and these bogs were created by old vegetation over the hundreds of years of compression. Anything that fell in to the bogs were so well preserved, sandals, humans, animals whatever they uncovered was surly intact, as it showed little age. Along the way back to the manor, Jerry the driver stopped along the road at this little shrine called the "Well of St Patrick's. We all got off the bus and took turns walking in to this small shrine, and of course there was water in this spring feed well, so I reached in and grabbed a hand full of rocks for keep sakes. Once I was on the bus, the women saw my rocks I picked up from the well; they wanted a rock from the well, so I shared my picking with them.

Later that evening we went down to the bar in the manor to chat and visit with the others from our group, sharing our personal history of our long lasting incredible journey that Debbie and I have successfully accomplished. We were so proud of our relationship with each other. Most people are taken back by our young age at marriage; we were proud and not a bit shy to admit it that we were truly kids at that time.

The next morning we boarded the bus and headed to Kilbeggen to stop and visit Lock's Distillery, this was very interesting, it was built in 1757. Where else can you go at 10:00am in the morning to have a whiskey tasting contest! What a blast, of course Debbie was not up to tasting the whiskey so I drank hers too.

From there we headed to Leap Castle, which is also known as Europe's most famous haunted site. This made our eyebrows lift up we were excited to experience this event. As we got to the castle gates I could not believe my eyes, we read about this castle before we came on this trip, and according to the history, this castle was built around 1640, one of the few true Irish castles intact and still standing. The brief history that was there were so many spirits in this castle lingered there. And in the 1930's they found a pit up in the Blood Chapel with a discolored square in the corner and once they broke through to see what was under this section, it was a dungeon loaded with bones and six foot spikes sticking out of the floor, so once you were thrown into this dungeon you would fall onto the spikes but apparently after a while the bodies were higher than the spikes, so their death had to be unbelievable. They emptied it out; it took three wagon loads of bones to clean this out.

In the 1994 I believe Sean Ryan purchased this property, along with this wife Ann and their daughter Keera. He had about half of the castle restored. They had their living area separate from the main lounging area where he entertained the guests. This was not a place you could stay at, it was a private home, but he allowed small groups to stop in and for €8 Euros per person he would give you the history of the castle, pour you a shot of Irish moonshine, and take about the spirits he and his family has experienced over the years. He played the tin whistle, as his daughter Keera would perform an Irish dance for us. She was amazing, she ranked one of the top four in the world for Irish dancing. She also played the harp sounded so sweet. The talent this family had was amazing! Our visit here at the castle was so short, I wanted to visit the Blood Chapel but at this time he was not allowing people up the short and narrow spiral staircase. As you were leaving the castle, Sean had CD's of his music for sale and we snatched one up and asked if he would autograph one for us, he was more than happy to do so.

As we left the castle and loaded onto the bus you could feel the enthusiasm from everyone's own personal experience with the castle. Debbie and I were blown away, and of course I picked up a rock from the yard as a souvenir from Leap Castle.

Our next stop was to Burr Castle, built in the eighteenth century, not quite as unique as "Leap", no comparison; this castle was a well known tourist attraction, nice to look at and walk around the city for a bit and head back to the manor. I remember we were taking a walk down the road from the manor to a local cemetery with this ruin church and with these graves dug in the middle of this ruin, with head stones from the 1700's. Very cool looking. As Debbie and I were walking around the ruin church she found this metal object and said, *"Dale look at this!"* It was a very old casket handle with Celtic designs on it, I dropped this into my pocket and took it back to our room and added it to my rock collection; I brought a sharpie marker with me so I wrote on every rock where it was picked up so I did not forget where I found it.

The next day we started heading to the Cliffs of Mother. Along the way we were to stop at the Mullingar Pewter factory too. After visiting the pewter factory we headed to the Cliffs! We made a short stop to the town of Doolin, to have lunch at the original Gus O' Connor's traditional pub.

Once we arrived at the Cliffs of Mother, it was a very clear day. We got" lucky". The view from the edge of this 700- foot drop off into the Atlantic Ocean was breath taking! I had to keep a close eye on Debbie so she would not to get too close to the edge. She trips sometimes and I could not let that happen. At this time there was not a wall built along the edge, you could walk right to the edge hang your feet it was amazing to see. I told Debbie I wanted a picture of looking over the edge, I told her I would be very careful, she did not want me to do it but I reassured her it would be fine. I got a wonderful picture over the edge. I believe this night we were scheduled to go on a pub crawl in Moth, a town not far from the manor. So that evening, we all loaded onto the tour bus and went into town. We went from pub to pub having a wonderful time! I remember we were in this pub and Debbie asks these two young men,

"How do you know so much history of your country?" He said to her, *"Pint by pint that's how we learn our history."*

I believe our last day we went to Kikenny City; it was the best preserved medieval town in Ireland. We visited a few churches, ate lunch and did quite a bit of shopping to take things back to the kids and friends. We did not want to go home, we were enjoying ourselves so much. The local were so friendly, we felt that we belonged here.

Well the next morning it was time for us to gather our belongings and board the bus, heading to Dublin Airport to go home. We talked about our experiences all the way home, and of course the people we met were all on this flight so we had plenty of people to chat with. This was a once in a life time event. We felt nothing could top this, later we will prove ourselves wrong. This was only the beginning of our adventures that lay ahead of us.

Once we arrived home it was time to come back to reality. The pictures we took were unbelievable to us. One in particular that caught our eyes was in Leap Castle in the upstairs parlor, it was a picture of Sean Ryan playing the tin whistle and sitting behind him on a couch was an older couple that was on our trip with us, but sitting next to them was a little girl and there were not young kids on the trip, it was all couples; that was unexplainable. So we started looking at all of out photos of Leap Castle and noticed a lot of orbs activity in the castle, especially in the Blood Chapel.

I was ready to plan our next vacation already. Debbie was the practical person, *"All in due time."* she would say. Well work continued on and our money was tight but we were getting by. Debbie was so good with money. We started going to Laughlin Arizona, probably once every month or two, and we loved Arizona. So we started thinking about buying a condo or something like that, something cheap we could afford. That was a tall order to fill. We could not find anything in our price range, so we started looking across the river in Bullhead City. We found this house in Lincoln Lane that was perfect, two bedrooms and a garage. This house had a sunroom that was the full length of the front of the house and the view was breath taking of the mountains. I believe we picked this up for around $72,000. Our payments were very low and Debbie knew she could swing it. And if she felt that I had no worries, she was a financial wizard. So we started taking things to the house in Arizona as we made trips up there. We bought furniture and kitchen needs.

After a while we were going there every other weekend and we were so excited about having our own home even if we did not live in it full time. We had a routine; every other Friday Debbie would take me to work. While I was working she would load up our Nissin Altima and at 2:30 pm she would be waiting outside my work door with Toto our dog, she is a mini pincher, the car was filled up with gas and we were ready to head to Arizona. We would hit the freeway just in between the Friday evening traffic. We would generally arrive in Bullhead City around 7:30pm. Open the house turn on the air conditioner, and feed the dog.

Then we would get back in the car and go over to Laughlin to have some fun for a while. Generally I have a few beers so Debbie would drive back to the house that night. The next day we would go to the breakfast at the Country Bears inn for some good old cooking before we started our day. Let me remind you Debbie is a fascinating cook, but this is our time to have fun and I really did not want her to mess with cleaning up at the house.

We would go to Oatman to do a little shopping and walking around, feed the donkeys carrots. Oatman was famous for the honeymoon night of Clark Gable and Carole Lombard; they stayed at the hotel here. The hotel was built around 1902 I believe and the honeymoon room that they stayed in is well preserved as it looked the night they stayed there. Debbie and I also liked collecting rocks, this was our favorite past time sounds goofy to a lot of people but we both truly loved doing this. We would venture out around Oatman and collect all kinds of thing, old car fan blades, found an old shovel next to an incomplete mine shaft, or just head out in to the desert looking for cool looking rocks. Debbie and I were so well matched with each other. GOD did a very wonderful thing when he brought her into my life. I could not of asked for anything more, GOD gave me the best.

We generally never planned our outing, we would just go. We enjoyed so many of the same things, and everything just fell into place without planning.

Work was still good but the money was not quite what I was use too in Michigan. In Michigan I was on the clock and could work all the over time I wanted, but here I was on salary and this created a fixed income.

We stayed busy in Laguna Nigel, we were about a couple of miles from the beach, and we both loved walking along the sea shore collecting sea shells, we had jars and jars of them. We actually took boxes of them to Arizona and put them in our front yard, for decoration.

For the next several months we were pretty much enjoying our life as always, going to Arizona every other week, hanging at the beach. We were trying so hard to save money so the next year we could go back to Ireland. I remember I was collecting all of the statehood quarters at that time. I told Debbie I will keep only five of each state and turn in the rest. But it only amounted to a few hundred dollars, not much help there. But Debbie was very good with money we always had enough, I still today cannot figure out how she was so good with money. She would go shopping for cloths and when I would come home from work she would say Dale I bet you cannot guess how much I paid for this blouse or these pants? I was always wrong; they were always less than I would guess. It would be a few dollars, she was so proud and pleased with her money saving and the great deals she would come across.

I do remember one day I was at work and received a call from Randy Bellestri, the owner of Odyssey, and was asking me about invar-36 material for bond tools, and I thought this was odd. Why would he, the owner of Global Tooling System and Odyssey Inc., be calling me just to talk about invar? I do know that they had a big problem with some tools they built for Spirit Air craft, and they did very badly with the tooling and lost a lot of money in the process. I did the same tools at Coast Composites and we made money and delivered them on time, so I was trying to read in between the lines of his conversation with me.

So when lunch time rolled around, I called Debbie and told her that Randy Bellestri called me and I think he might want me to come back to Odyssey. *"What do you think Debbie? Do you want to see what he has to offer, if I am right?"* Debbie said, *"Sure I'm ready to go back if the money is right and they pay for our move."*

So I thought about it and the next day as I was taking my walk during lunch at work, I did this everyday just to get out of my chair and stretch. I called Randy on my cell phone and asked him if he was interested in me coming back to Odyssey, of course he was very interested. He was very aware of my talent and experience in the fabrication of aircraft tooling. I told him I would talk to Debbie and call him later that night. Of course I called Debbie right away and said, *"Let's talk about this when I get home and let's come up with a number for the money and what else we would like them to do for us."* One thing was for Odyssey to pay for our move too.

So once I got home from work, we were talking about the money, and I came up with this high number, Debbie said, "Randy won't go for that!" I said, *"Well he could talk me down a bit, might as well go for the most and except less."* I called Randy and said, *"This is what I need my salary to be at."* I gave him a number, and I would like for Odyssey to pay for my moving expenses too.

He said let me talk to Jeff Hutton and I will call you back, I believe the next day he called and accepted my terms. I looked at Debbie and she could not believe I got what I asked for, she was so happy. I told Randy I needed about a month to pack and settle things here and I gave him a date of Nov.24, 2005, I will start work. We had a lot to do to make this happen. The saddest part was our house in Arizona, we knew that we could not keep it and move back to Michigan too. The distance was too far for us to maintain, so we got a realtor to put our house up for sale. Believe it or not our house sold within a couple of months and we doubled our money on this house.

Debbie did a wonderful job packing. She had a lot of practice in packing over the years of our marriage. We shipped her Nissan Altima to Michigan and we drove my Nissan Xterra to Michigan, along with our dog Toto, she has been with us forever, it seems.

This is in November of 2005 we made this trip. We did a lot of stopping along the way, not in too big of a hurry. One of the deals I had with Odyssey was my medical insurance started right away, so no worries there. We did stop at my stepmom's house to meet her new husband, the second one after my dad died. He was a very nice and gentle man; he even persuaded my stepmom to give me my father's flag that was draped over his casket at the military funeral. That was very nice of him I cherished this flag very much.

Once we arrived in Lake Orion Debbie noticed a chip in my windshield and she said, *"Dale you watch that chip will crack right across your windshield."* *"No it won't."* I said. No more than 1 minute later, all of a sudden you could actually hear my windshield crack all the way across, she was right once again like usual.

We were staying at the extended stay hotel, you pay by the week and you have a kitchen with all of the cooking needs: plates, cups, everything you need. We also called our friends Karen and Gary Laible to let them know that we were back so we could start spending time together again. Karen and Gary are like family we have known for so long; it was nice to see them again. Debbie and Judy Middleton start up where they left off with their friendship, like we never left.

So I start working again at Odyssey just before thanksgiving 2005, in the meantime, Debbie was looking for a home close to my work, which I was very happy about that and Lake Orion is a very nice area, close to shopping at the Great Lakes Crossing mall, Freeway I-75 right there. She was looking into the "Kedington Meadows" development. We wanted something close to the lake but then we thought during the weather you would get a cold breeze blowing across the frozen lake. Anyway the price at that time was high and we were not too sure if we were willing to pay a lot.

So Debbie and I were driving around in the neighborhood on Ashley Drive and at the end of the street before the road made a left turn, was this two story brick home. We drove up to it and it had a for sale sign in the yard. We thought by looking at the outside it most likely would be out of our price range. Debbie called the realtor's number on the sign anyway and they told us what the house was going for and we were so surprised, we could afford this house with no problem.

We scheduled a day to do a walk through and this house was built in the early eighties. It showed it was owned by a pastor of a church and they were moving on to a new adventure. I knew this house could not have any unwanted spirits with a pastor living there. And of course Debbie looked beyond the appearance of the house and was able to visualize her own expectations of what the house could look like with a bit of decorating and elbow grease, that's where I come in at. We made an offer on the house and everything went well. It was a bi-level brick house with a gable awning hanging over the porch, with two columns one in each corner, and four windows in front with plastic shutters.

When you entered the house you could either go upstairs or downstairs to the den. Upstairs was the kitchen, bathroom, two bedrooms, a sitting room and dining room and a sliding glass door on to a 12ft x 18ft wooden deck. Down stairs were the laundry room, a bathroom, two bedrooms, a very large den, and a sliding door out to the backyard.

After working on removing all the carpet from downstairs and while Dylan was with us, he put down the wooden floor for us. He did a wonderful job in the den that we had him do the hallway and one of the bedrooms downstairs. In the meantime, Debbie and I started painting the downstairs den. We wanted to get a fence around our back yard for Toto the rotten min pin, which keeps going. So we had our backyard surveyed for a fence and come to find out we had a pie shape yard that was about ½ acre, more yard then we wanted, funny to say, but I really do not care for yard work that much. We had a chain link fence put up so Toto could not get out of the yard.

We were getting settled in with this house, things were coming together very nicely and my four mile drive to work was awesome. This location was making it easier for us to go to see the kids in Wisconsin. Debbie was so excited that we could drive to Riverside outside of Chicago. So the first opportunity we had we drove there to see Joshua and Heidi, they are such a match made in heaven, and we could not ask for a better daughter-in-law, we love her very much and she fitted in with us all so well. Joshua was a conductor on the railroad and it was a great job, he loves it. Debbie would bring up the fact that when we lived in Huntington Beach, California, Joshua was in high school and he would wear overalls to school with tie-dye tee shirts. I guess he had the railroad in his blood at a young age.

We were doing well taking trips over the border into Canada, going to the casinos at Point Edwards, and sometimes continuing on to Niagara Falls to see Karen and Gary. Or we would just go to the casinos on a Sunday just to get out for a bit. Debbie started bowling with her old tea mates and they were so glad to have her again. She started a Bunko group with some of our local neighbors and she also was a substitute with her old Bunko group. The reason she did not stay with the old group was because of the distance, it was quite far for her to drive every week. We started going to concerts here locally DTE and the Palace, they were within ten minutes e from our house and we were seeing some real good performers. I was getting a little spoiled. Nothing in California was close to what we had here. DTE is an outdoor venue, sit on the grass or pay a little bit more and pavilion sitting. We had seen some great performers there from Ringo Starr to Eric Clapton, Randy Travis, Badfinger, actually after Badfinger performed I wanted a beer and Debbie needed to visit the restroom. So while I was waiting for Debbie, I looked over to the beer booth and standing there was Joey Molland the singer for Badfinger and I said to Debbie "watch this" I walked over to him and said, *"Thanks for all of the wonderful years of the music that you gave me thru the years growing up."* His face lit up with a big smile and Debbie and I was just carrying on a pretty good conversation with him, and I guess it was his manager who said, *"We need to go."* I said would it be alright if my wife takes our picture together and he said it was perfectly fine.

The Palace front row: Paul McCartney, Bob Dylan, Bob Seger as well as a lot of Piston games. I was getting tickets quite often and Debbie would go down to the Palace box office on discount days, half price tickets, we were doing pretty good, but was not feeling like this was our home

We decided to go back to Ireland in 2006, I believe it was around February and we got a fantastic deal for that time of the year. We flew to Ireland with the same Harp and Eagle tour. When we landed in Ireland, Declan was there and greeted us and he had this very surprising look on his face to see us come back! Of course Peter had move on, so we had a different driver. We still had a fabulous time and we met some wonderful people. Of course our enthusiasm was going to be the day we get to go back to Leap Castle!

Now I need to give you a little back ground on our last trip to Ireland. We were at Leap Castle and Shawn Ryan was playing the tin whistle for us all and I took a picture of him and in the background sitting next to an old couple that we met was a blonde little girl, this struck us rather odd because there were no kids in our group and we had never seen her.

So we made an 8x10 photo of this and took it to Ireland so we could give it to Shawn Ryan. So once we arrived at Leap Castle and while he was giving the history of the castle we presented the photo to him and he was very fascinated with the photo so we gave it to him to have. And Keera his daughter was going to the states for a Celtic dancing competition. Debbie gave Shawn €50 euro for her to have for her trip. It was not a lot of money but he was very pleased to give it to her. On this day we went to Trim Castle where "Braveheart", the movie with Mel Gibson star in, was filmed at. This was a very large castle and we enjoyed this very much even though it was cloudy and cold, it is February. We still enjoyed this trip very much. We knew we could never go wrong going to Ireland, what a wonderful country and the people are just as wonderful as their country.

After returning home for this wonderful vacation, things got back to our normal routine, working and Debbie was starting to get into the "art of pottery." She was starting to spend time in Rochester Hill and this painted pot gallery and was becoming very enthusiastic making pottery. She was so busy with bowling, Bunko and pottery she had no time on her hands and that was very nice, she was really never bored.

We had done a few trips to Canada and pretty much kept on our routine for a while, we had no real interesting things going on. Debbie was fighting the fibromyalgia and she was going to the doctors and she kept changing doctors because they would blame the problem she was having on the fibromyalgia, she just did not believe that all of her problems were based on just the particular diagnose. See Debbie would look up all of the symptoms and she was very much in tune with her body, this lady was very intelligent to say the least. She would get very disgusted with not being able to find the proper doctor that would listen to her. So she went about her life and handled the discomfort the best she could, you see she really never complained much she just bared with it.

We kept in touch with my nephew Terry and his wife Julie, they were close to us. Debbie and Terry stayed in contact over the years, we felt like he was one of our sons, that's how good we felt connected. I remember Terry and Julie were living in Athens, Greece around 2007, they asked, *"Why you don't come here and visit us on your next vacation and we will show you around?"* We said that might work so Debbie and I pondered the ideal of going to Greece. So we looked on the internet and checked for warnings of American tourists, and there really weren't any. We started researching what is in Athens and we were blown away with the age of the city and the Romans and Greek ruins. We spoke with Jack and Bobbie almost every weekend. You see Jack has been a brother to me for the last forty-three years; we went to grade school together.

We spoke many times about going on vacation together but never worked out. So while we were on the phone one weekend and we mentioned that we were thinking about going to Greece to see Terry and Julie. Jack said let's plan on going together, what a fabulous idea! So Debbie and Jack (mister squeaky butt better known as beyond thrifty), were planning the trip. We told Terry and Julie that our friends Jack and Bobbie were joining us on this trip. So we were in the planning stages of how we were going to make this happen without over loading Terry and Julie with guests. You see they have two boys, Wade and Bret. We decided to get a hotel in the Plaka area in Athens at the Hera or the Hadrian Hotel. So we decided to stay five days in Athens with Jack and Bobbie because they want to go to Germany for a few days, so we were to go and stay with Terry and Julie for a few days before returning to the states.

You see Jack and Bobbie live in Denver and we live in Michigan so we decided to meet up in Athens and my nephew Terry would pick us all up at the airport. We lift Detroit airport to Charles de Gaulle airport. Once we landed at the airport, they were under heavy reconstruction, so by the time we got from one end of the airport to the other, we missed our flight. So Debbie went up to the counter and said to the ticket agent that we missed our flight and as soon as Debbie started to speak he realized we were American's, he started having attitude. Debbie told him she made sure if we miss the flight we would be booked on the next flight to Athens. He said that true you will need to wait until tomorrow as he is typing on his keyboard, that he said with a sarcastic tone, *"I see it. Oh I guess you are booked on the next flight."*

We did our best to just get to the gate and wait for our next flight. I tried to call Jack on this international phone with no luck trying to let him know we were going to be late and Terry did not know what Jack and Bobbie looked like, this was starting to become a fiasco.

Once we landed in Athens we saw jack and Bobbie by chance, and then we ran into Terry, he had left and came back for the next flight coming from France. So this all worked out fine. We got into Terry's van which he had shipped from the states, this was a full size van and maneuvering through the narrow streets of Athens was a challenge in itself let alone the crazy drivers and all the scooters.

Once we arrived at our Hotel in the Plaka district, we had reservations at the Herdon Hotel and Terry drop us off and said we will meet up later in that evening for dinner. Debbie and I were so glad to see Terry, it had been a very long time since we have seen him. We checked into our rooms and when I opened our blinds in the room, the view was so breath taking, there stood the "Parthenon on top of the Acropolis" the Parthenon is a temple on top of the Athenian Acropolis, dedicated to the Greek goddess Athena.

It wasn't too far away either, what a view we had. After checking in and resting a bit, we decided to go around the area for dinner and sightseeing. As we walked around the Plaka area and the base of the Acropolis it was so incredible, we sat down at this small restaurant and enjoyed "real" Greek food for the first time and I enjoyed it so much with a glass of Osseo and I'm happy, it had a taste like black licorice, it had a high alcohol content.

The people in the Plaka area, was very well spoken with the English language, this help a lot being able to communicate with the locals. Terry and Julie knew a lot of the local restaurant managers so we were treated like royalty at these places, they would take us into the kitchen to try different items. What a great experience we had. Before we left the states I got a hold of a limousine service in Athens to take all of us to Delphi, this location was dedicated to Apollo, Oracle, Delphic Sibyl. This is one of the most important archaeological sites in Greece.

Between the sixth and fourth centuries BC, the Delphic oracle, which was regarded as the most trustworthy was at its peak. It was delivered by the Pythia, the priestess, and interpreted by the priests of

Apollo. Cities, rulers and ordinary individuals alike consulted the oracle, expressing their gratitude with great gifts and spreading its fame around the world. The oracle was thought to have existed since the dawn of time. Indeed, it was believed to have successfully predicted events related to the cataclysm of Deukalion, the Argonaut's expedition and the Trojan War; more certain are the consultations over the founding of the Greek colonies. It was the oracle's fame and prestige that caused two Sacred Wars in the middle of the fourth and fifth centuries BC. In the third century BC, the sanctuary was conquered by the Aetolians, who were driven out by the Romans in 191 BC. In Roman times, the sanctuary was favored by some emperors and plundered by others, including Sulla in 86 BC.

The rise of the Rationalist movement in philosophy in the third century BC, damaged the oracle's authority, yet its rituals continued unchanged into the second century AD, when it was consulted by Hadrian and visited by Pausanias. The latter's detailed description of the buildings and more than three hundred statues have greatly contributed to our reconstruction of the area. The Byzantine emperor Theodosius finally abolished the oracle and the Slavs destroyed the precinct in 394 BC. With the advent of Christianity, Delphi became an episcopal see, but was abandoned in the sixth-seventh centuries AD. Soon after, in the seventh century AD, a new village, Kastri, grew over the ruins of the ancient sanctuary, attracting, in modern times, several travelers interested in antiquities.

Archaeological research in Delphi began in 1860 by Germans. In 1891, the Greek government granted the French School at Athens permission for long-term excavations on the site. It is then that the village of Kastri was removed to allow for the so-called "Great Excavation' to take place. The Great Excavation uncovered spectacular remains, including about three thousand inscriptions of great importance for our knowledge of public life in ancient Greece. Today, the Greek Archaeological Service and the French School at Athens continue to research, excavate and conserve the two Delphic sanctuaries. Of all the monuments, only the Treasury of the Athenians had enough of its original building material preserved to allow for its almost complete reconstruction. The project was financed by the City of Athens and carried through by the French

School in 1903-1906. The Chiot altar, the Temple of Apollo and the Tholos were also partially restored. In 1927 and 1930, the poet Angelos Sikelianos and his wife, Eva, attempted to revive the Delphic idea and make of Delphi a new cultural centre of the earth, through a series of events that included performances of ancient theatre.

As we were walking around Delphi I always scanned the ground looking for relics, rocks, and chard pottery and as I was, here in Greece you are not allowed to pick anything up from the ground, they have these people that are either up on hills or behind areas so you cannot see them and if you bend down to pick something up, you will hear them blowing a whistle and you can get into some real trouble. So as I was walking I saw this piece of pottery sticking out of this hillside and I causally grab it as I was walking by and got away with it. These are the type of souvenirs that Debbie and I always looked for.

This limousine service was very nice and no one had to be burdened by driving, I believe it was at least a two or three hour drive one way from Athens.

We were so amazed just walking the city. The history here was fascinating; from Roman ruins to the ancient Greek ruins. We went to this jewelry store in the Plaka area at this place were Julie shopped for her jewelry, so Debbie and I were looking around for something to buy, either matching rings or something. And then this necklace caught her eye, it was in the form of the Greek pattern, it was 18 k gold and the owner of the store gave us a very good price so I bought it for my Debbie. Debbie's face had this glow of happiness, and she was most definitely walking on clouds that afternoon and as we walked by other jewelry stores the people at the stores would say they have a bracelet to match that necklace, so finally she asked, *"Ok, how much for the bracelet?"* the jeweler asked *"How much did you pay for the necklace?"* and Debbie said, *"€$800.00 euro's."* he said, *"No way did you pay that for a necklace, like I want to know who sold that to you."* and Debbie refused to say, I believe that was how much or close to that he was going to charge for the bracelet . This piece of jewelry had become one of the most photographed photos of her with this necklace on, she absolutely loved it, and I was so glad I bought it for her.

We also went to the Temple of Olympian Zeus and Hadrian's Arch where I found all of ancient pieces of clay pottery of drainage systems, and of course inconspicuously picked up pieces and put them into Bobbie's bag she was carrying. I thought she was going to freak-out, I told her don't worry about it, no one had seen me pick these up, do you hear a whistle blow? I believe the next day we were scheduled to go on our cruise to visit the three islands in the Mediterranean Sea, it was a one day trip to the islands, Aegina, Poros, and Agistri, all three islands were so beautiful, I'm not sure which one of the three island you could only ride donkeys, no cars and Debbie said I want to go on a donkey ride and to tell you the truth, it was a very enjoyable journey. Debbie said, *"Dale this is so cool, I love this!"*

After the five days were up, Jack and Bobbie were flying to Germany and we were to stay a few days with Terry and Julie. We had a wonderful time with them, they are "family" and Wade, what a smart young man, and Beret was just a little guy. Debbie loves holding babies so she had no problem sitting around holding the baby.

Well it was time to leave Greece. Terry dropped us off at the airport and we were on our way home, but we had the same time frame in France and we thought that we would most likely miss our connecting flight. So we thought we might spend a day in Paris if we did not make our connection. And as we're flying low over Paris we got the most spectacular view of the Eiffel Tower. That I thought was enough of Paris. So once our plane landed this man was holding a sign with our name "Weatherford" on it, we said we are the Weatherford's, so he got us in this car and drove us over to our plane so we would not miss our connecting flight.

Once we were back home and back to our normal routine, Debbie always had a spark of interest in pottery, so she started going to the" Painted Pot" in Rochester, Michigan right off of main street. Julian was the owner and she and Debbie connected right away. So now Debbie has this hobby and she was determined to perfect it as she does with everything she gets involved with, because after a few times making her bowls and design baskets, she was hooked.

She was still on her bowling league every Wednesday and Bunko and now pottery. She was so busy she did not have time to work, and that's the way I wanted it.

I remember one afternoon Joshua and Heidi called and said that they were going to have a baby!

Debbie and I were so excited to become grandparents. Debbie went to Lacrosse, Wisconsin to visit Joshua and Heidi when she had the time this was so great for the both of us. We just needed to wait and see when the date gets closer and try to be there when the little baby arrives.

I do remember one afternoon we were in the spa in the back yard, and Debbie said that she and Julian wanted to open a new business. Julian wanted to sell the Painted Pot and move over onto Main Street in Rochester, this is a very busy and historic town, more geared for the upper class society.

Debbie said Julian could not do this by themselves; she wanted Debbie to be her partner. So I thought this was a wonderful idea. Debbie loved pottery and now she and Julian were going to open a pottery studio and art gallery. So they started looking for an empty store on Main Street and just by chance there was this antique store that was closing after twenty years or more of business. I remember walking into the store; it was part on the old Masonic temple from the early 1800's. This place was perfect, right in the heart of the busiest portion of Main Street. The ceiling had the old tin stamp designs like tiles, old brick walls with arches; Debbie had a vision of local artist displaying their work in the front portion and in the windows of the store, and a working class beyond the gallery. So when people came in they would see the art and also see pottery being developed in the back. Down stairs would be where all of the supplies would be kept, the glazes as well as the kiln for "firing up" the pottery.

We met with the owner one night, he was a doctor at Starbucks Coffee shop, and we signed a lease for two years and then after that if the gallery was doing well we would sign back up. We were so excited to get this business off the ground, so once the lease was up and the antiques were moved out, we started to redesign the floor plan by removing an office to open up the floor space. We removed the carpet and repainted the molding to a burgundy color. Debbie said, *"Dale, I came up with a name for the store, how do you like "Firebrick Gallery?"*

I absolutely loved it so her and Julian went to a sign making shop and had the sign made. so Before it was put up, we painted the front of the store with burgundy and the lettering was gold color, it really popped out.

So Debbie was on a mission to contact local artists for displaying their work. Debbie and I would go to art and craft fairs and if Debbie liked their work she would introduce herself and let them know of their new gallery called "Firebrick Gallery' opening soon in Rochester on Main Street, she would tell them if they would like to display their work.

Every artist that came to the gallery fell in love with the way the gallery was set up, and was more than happy to have their work on display for sale on consignment with the gallery. They had artist work on canvas, pottery, jewelry, and photos. We knew this was going to be a hit on opening day! We put a lot of hard work and late nights working on laying down fiber board for the floor and varnishing it, and redoing the restroom. We gave this place a face lift from the ground up with all of this coming together for the grand opening day June 27, 2008.

In the meantime our grandson Miles Liam came into the world on April 26th, 2008 at 7:08 pm, weighing 9lbs 12oz, 21in. long.
Debbie wanted to wait until Heidi got home from the hospital with Miles before she would make her journey to Lacrosse to help Heidi at home. I remember going to" Babies R us" with Debbie and we were like new parents buying thing for our child! I told Debbie I would prefer for her to fly to their house, but she insisted on driving to save a few hundred dollars. I was always so worried when she made long drives alone; I was very protective of her well being. I did not want anything to go wrong, or put her in harms way. I do believe she spent two weeks with Joshua, Heidi and Miles. Debbie loved every moment of it with her first new grandson. After she returned from Lacrosse Wisconsin, we went back to work on her new adventure, the pottery studio.

Opening Day was an unbelievable turn out; it was so crowed inside the gallery that night, you could hardly move around, it was a home run hit for them; it could not have gone any better!
Debbie and Julian were so proud of what they had accomplished!

Debbie was so happy and getting more and more interested in learning different techniques of build and creating different ideas for making ceramics. She started taking large leaves, pressing them into the clay and forming leaf bows as well as cups and bowls. After a while she was looking for a kiln to put in our back patio so she could create at home as well. I told her to buy a new one but she insisted on a used one. What was strange about that was when she was looking for a used one; she found one that someone had for sale around the corner. We bought it and got it home, it was an old one but large enough to do large leaf bowls and other items. I had an electrician come out and wire it for 240 volts and had the main plug in right by the kiln.

I would go up to the gallery every night to be with Debbie while she was work and then help clean up and then I would follow her home. Sometimes we did not get out of there until 11:00 pm or so. I did not mind this at all, Debbie was happy and I was as well. Just seeing the dedication she had, love she had for this art, she made me very proud!

Debbie was working very hard with the studio and her own projects at home and of course her bowling league every Wednesday morning and Bunko every month, she stayed very active. It made me tired just watching her buss around. We were content with our lives, a lot of time we never had to say a word to each other, just being together was satisfying.

For Debbie's fiftieth birthday she wanted nothing but to spend her birthday with her grandson Miles. So let me give you a bit of history about fiftieth birthdays. When Bobbie turned fifty, we surprised her by flying to Colorado for her birthday. For my Birthday, Jack and Bobbie flew to Detroit for my fiftieth, and then for Jack's fiftieth we spent it in Niagara –on –the –lake, Canada. So for Debbie's, Jack and Bobbie flew to Lacrosse Wisconsin to Josh and Heidi's, so this was a tradition for the four of us on our fiftieth to spend together.

You see Jack and Bobbie, we grew up pretty much together, and we have a very tight bond with our family and theirs. I don't want to hurt anyone's feeling but we were not closer to any other family then the Weavers. Karen and Gary Laible I do have to say we love them very much, we just lost connections every now and then but never left our hearts, and when we got together it seemed like we never lost connection, if you can understand that type of love and friendship.

So we flew to Lacrosse Wisconsin and Debbie was so happy. You see Debbie was this light that is unexplainable, she actually had a glow about her, everyone who came in contact with her thought she was a wonderful person, and she always was and to me still is. We had a very wonderful time with everyone; you see we really never had any drama in our small circle of family, we made sure of it. After returning home we decided that we needed to buy a home in Arizona, mainly the property value of homes were dropping and so Debbie started looking on reality.com for short sales on homes. In the meantime Dylan was doing a bit of research of his own on where were good places to buy around Phoenix and he stumbled up on a city called Queen Creek, Arizona. So this is where Debbie started looking at homes. She contacted a realtor in that area and set up a weekend that we would fly out there and look for a winter home that Debbie could spend the winters there. You see Debbie had so much pain in the winters and it was hard for the fibromyalgia she had, and it saddened me to see her suffer, and we both loved Arizona. So we flew to Arizona, met the realtor and spent all day looking at trashed houses and we were getting very discouraged, and we were running out of time before we needed to go home. That's when she said, *"Ok we've looked at all of these homes and now I want you to come with me to a new development of homes."* Mine and Debbie's first thought was now we are really wasting our time. So we went to Rancho Bella Vista development and were looking at new homes and the price was not bad at all for a new home. We found this single level home that both of us fell in love with, with all up grades, built in appliances, 1526 sq. feet and ceramic tile floors, absolutely wonderful!

Needless to say we bought this house and all the free time I got, we were in Arizona. The yard was dirt front and back so we knew we had some landscaping that needed to be done.

After our return from Arizona we went back to our normal routine, I working at Odyssey and her at the gallery. I knew that the gallery was taking its toll on Debbie; I knew that she and Julian were growing apart. I remember one evening we were out on the patio and she said that she was no longer happy with the way things were going at the gallery and she wanted out, she started crying and said, *"I didn't want to let you down Dale.*" I said, "*Debbie you not letting me down, you gave it a go and you created a wonderful business you should be proud, if this is not what you want to do any more then get out of it and move on with your own creations, I'm here to back you up.*" her happiness was the one thing that always touched my soul.

She continued with her pottery, we converted one of our bedrooms into a studio for her, bought a potter's wheel, slab roller and whatever she needed to continue on with her pottery. She created the most amazing pieces at home, her imagination was so creative. We did not know what her pieces would look like until they came out of the kiln. But to me everything she created I loved, I was a bad judge probably because if she made it I loved it, it was a part of her own creation and I love everything about her and her mind.

Her next adventure was a travel agent and of course she worked hard with that and she liked it because she could work from home and still do the things she loved to do. She studied and got her travel agent license, so she started booking trips for friends and clients. See Debbie is a people person and she loved meeting people and talking, she could talk to anyone and was good at it.

So when winter rolled around Debbie would take off around the first of December and return to our house in Arizona, with our house being new she needed to add the "Debbie" touch. She repainted the house, had the yard landscaped and what a wonderful job she did with that. The first year she went Debbie asked, "*Do you want me to make you dinners before I leave?*" I said no I will be fine and off course I ate like really bad, mostly because I do not cook, so there was a lot of eating out in the three months she was gone. But I would fly out to Arizona at Christmas and spend New Year's with her and then I would go home back to work. Of course I missed her a lot when she was in Arizona but she felt so good being away from the winters of Michigan. I did not mind her going there.

I was always so excited to pick her up when she came home! I know she would love to stay there all the time but she missed me as well, we could not move there because I had a great paying job that allowed us to live like we do. There was no aircraft tooling companies in Arizona. So we did our best to deal with our life style, going back and forth and we were happy about that.

Debbie and I wanted to go on another vacation, and we picked Italy this time. Called up Jack and Bobbie our traveling companions, and they wanted to go with us and we thought this would be great! So between Debbie and "mister tight wad Jack", we were able to plan a wonderful vacation, first Rome, Florence and then Tuscany. We planned this so we could spend our thirty-eight wedding anniversary in Italy, Debbie always dreamed of going to Tuscany, and now we are going there!

So Debbie was getting ready to go to Arizona for the winter, she said, *"I'm going to start cooking for you and I will label everything for you so all Dale would need to do is pop it in the microwave and have dinner."* I did not argue with her because I was looking forward to good meals this winter while she was going to be gone. She cooked, and wrap -up seventy-five dinners and placed them in our deep freezer for me while she would be gone. She always took very good care of me.

When December 2010 rolled around I flew to Arizona and we had a wonderful time, even with my over drinking at the hotel the night before my flight to Arizona, she was a bit upset with me but we did alright handling that, I was a bit embarrassed with myself for my action that night.

After returning from Arizona, I was so excited about our trip to Italy, Debbie was leaving Arizona to come home and pack up for our Italy trip. She really was not ready to come home so soon, she was enjoying herself so much there. I was remembering waiting in the baggage claim department for Debbie's arrival. I was so excited to see her walking to the baggage claim, "my baby is home again" I thought. This was mid March 2011 and our trip was scheduled for March 30th – April 10th. We planned this so we could spend our thirty-eighth wedding anniversary on April seventh in Italy.

Once we had everything packed and ready to go, we were scheduled to fly to Newark, meet Jack and Bobbie, and change flights to Rome. Once we landed in Rome we had the hotel shuttle pick us up and drive us to the hotel. I was so fascinated as we drove by some of the most spectacular sights, the Coliseum and the aqueduct and ancient ruins everywhere, unbelievable!

Once we arrived at our hotel and got to our room, Debbie and I just lay down on our bed and were out like a light. When we woke up a few hours later we were ready to hit the town. So I called Jack and Bobbie's room and they had a bit of trouble with their shower and had to change rooms and they were just getting ready to take a nap. So Debbie and I headed down the street looking for some place to eat dinner and catch some local sights. Truly amazing as we were walking down the street, the sun was setting; lots of people walking, streets were busy with scooters and small automobiles. We walked to the center of the roundabout and noticed a lot of cafés and we were trying to decide which one to eat at. Until this man in front of the café came up to us and was very nice letting us know that they make their own pasta fresh and reassured us we would not regret eating there. So we went in and sat down. He brought us Champagne and took our order. We were trying to decide what wine we wanted to have and as we looked along the wall we noticed Refino brand and we asked about this wine and he said it was a very popular wine and was locally bottled, sounded good to us so I ordered a bottle and Debbie asked, *"Are you sure we want a bottle?"* *"Yes we will drink, we are in Italy."* I remember the waiter came over and gave Debbie a freshly cut rose. She was so in the "moment", the glimmer in her eyes was so breath taking for me, she was so happy. After dinner we just started walking down the street and found my favorite place the "Hard Rock Café", of course I had the venture inside, got a few shirts and bought Miles, our grandson, a jacket. So it was getting late so we headed back to our hotel to call it a night.

The next morning we wanted to get to the Vatican so we headed to the main street where the hotel guest information told us where to go. We stopped at this little café for coffee, but in Italy they do not drink much coffee and we had a hard time communicating with the locals, English language is not spoken often. So we were able to get an espresso and purchase tickets for the local bus 64 to get us to the Vatican.

Once we arrived at the Vatican it was very early in the morning and there was no line to get into the Vatican. We actually walked right in. What breathe taking architecture, it was unreal! We were so taken away by the beauty you really cannot describe it in words. I remember Debbie was having a bit of trouble with needing to use the restrooms more often than usual and like "right now" type situation. But we thought it was nothing to be too concerned with, we just made sure we were able to find one when she needed it and she thought that once we get home she was surly going to talk to her doctor.

After visiting the Vatican we caught the on-hop – hop off bus and headed over to the Pantheon, built A.D.117-138, I really wanted to view this amazing structure. We visited the Roman Forum; Bath of Caracalla built in A.D.211, and Palantine Hill. Debbie's favorite was the famous Trevi Fountain! I remember going there after dinner and the square was so crowded we really could not get any good photos. So we decided to come back early in the morning to take photos. The next morning we walked to it from our hotel, that was not far at all, and was able to capture so many fabulous photos, even Debbie throwing a coin over her shoulder into the fountain, meaning you will return again.

We had planned to only spend a couple of days in Rome; from there we went to Florence, actually called Firenze. What was so funny was trying to buy the tickets from Rome to Florence at the train station; the city of Florence did not exist in the ticket machine. Jack, Bobbie and I sat back and if anyone could figure out this ticket machine, Debbie would be the one and of course she was smarter than the ticket machining and we were on our way to Firenze, we call Florence; while we were there we did a tour called the "Best of Tuscany." We visited an organic farm and were able to enjoy some of the best wines from the area that was actually made from the grapes grown at this farm. We went to Siena, San Gimignano, Pisa, to see the leaning tower of Piza. It one of the most spectacular tours we ever been on and the guide was very nice, spoke perfect English.

We were so fascinated with the Italy trip, but of course every good vacation has to come to an end sooner or later. Once we got back home Debbie went back to the doctors to try and figure out why she was feeling like she had vertical issues along with her bladder control. She had told Dr. Harding what was going on and she gave Debbie some medication for the bladder problem and that seemed to help with that problem.

So for the fourth of July we decided to go and visit our friends Karen and Gary in Niagara Falls for that weekend. We had a wonderful time visiting them and seeing the fireworks one night sitting in a parking lot with a bottle of wine, just like in the old times with them in the seventies.

Debbie and I did so much walking that weekend and she started noticing that her left shoe was catching the pavement every once in a while, we thought it was her shoes, not thinking of anything else. Also while we were at Fort Niagara we were standing on a little hill and Debbie was feeling dizzy she had to sit down.

Once we got home she started to get a little vertical, she had this before but for some reason this time seemed a bit different. She went in to see Dr. Harding. Dr Harding gave Debbie medication for the vertical, but after taking the medication for a while it was not working she was getting worst.

Debbie went back to Dr Harding letting her know that she was not feeling any better, Debbie also told her the she was seeing a chiropractor. So Dr Harding said let's do an MIR with on her brain "contrast", this is a dye that in injected into the blood stream to help intensify the visualization in her brain.

I needed to go to California for work and Debbie was ok with driving right now. I went with her for the MRI and they said that the report would be sent to her Doctor after the results come in. So in the mean time I left for California for a meeting with Boeing and Coast Composite. Odyssey and Coast were teamed up for a larger program for Boeing.

I remember sitting in the conference room at Coast with Boeing, this is around 10:00 am my phone started ringing and I look and it was Debbie, now Debbie knew that I was in a very important meeting, so I thought this has to be very important for her to call. I stood up and answered the phone as I was walking out of the conference room. Hello Debbie I said, and she was crying on the phone I said what's the matter and she said that she got the report back on her MRI and they found lesions on her brain, she said *"Dale I don't want to die!"* My heart just shattered in to pieces, I told her I would leave right now for the airport and come home she said please come home to night please!

I walked into the meeting room and closed my laptop. I said there is an emergency at home I need to leave. I went straight to the airport and caught a flight home that evening.

Once I got home Debbie said, "Dr. Harding wanted her to go see neurologist to determine what the lesions are caused from."

So the next day we went to the neurologist, the doctor look at the x-rays and said he believes that she has MS but wanted to have more tests done. First he wanted her to go in and have a spinal tap to draw some fluid from the spine and test it for cancer. So we went to hospital and had the procedure done, they sent to the lab and we waited for the results that would come in a few days. Well the lab messed up and we were told that the procedure would need to be done again.

So we made another appointment for this to be done; now we needed to wait again for the results. Well the results came back negative for cancer; we were so relieved it's not cancer! We were not happy about MS but it was not life threatening, we could deal with that. So the neurologist wanted her to start IV steroids twice a day for a week, he said this will shrink the lesions. At this time we put our faith in whatever he wanted us to do. So he set up an appointment for a nurse to come to our house to hook up a port in her vein and showed me how to start the IV in the evening. We did this for a week and then we went back to the neurologist and he wanted to send her in for another MRI to see if the steroids reduced the lesions. After the doctor got the results back he said that something was not right, he said the lesions did not shrink they got quite a bit larger and there was more of them! By this time Debbie was starting to be a wall walker, leaning against the wall while walking up and down the stairs. She seems to be getting worse every day. The doctor started her on the medication and she had to get injections in her leg, I was watching her doing these injections so I could do them for her. The first injection she was sitting on the edge of the bed, I was so proud of her she did it like a pro with no hesitation right in the leg. We were supposed to spend her fifty-third birthday at our home in Arizona (August 8th), but there was no way we could go in her condition. I took her to her favorite place to eat Cracker Barrel, after that I went to Motor City casino that was a very fine day.

She did this for about a week, and each day she would worsen, we kept waiting for the meds to kick in but didn't.

So we went back to the neurologist and he said we need to put you in the hospital and run some tests, but he said, "He is sticking to MS."

On August 10th she was admitted into St Joseph Mercy Oakland, in Pontiac for more tests. On August 12th she came home. She continued the meds and nothing was helping her she no longer could drive, she also was having trouble walking without holding on to me. I was so worried, hoping for the best as long as I could do whatever it took to help her. I was worried about leaving her at home by herself when I would go to work.

I put up a rail in the shower for her to hold onto during her showers, she would call me when she got in and call me when she got out of the shower so I would know she was fine (she would place it on the lid of the toilet so it was handy for her).

On August 16th Debbie got into to the shower and she had fallen, lucky she was able to reach her phone to call me. She said, *"Dale I fell in the shower and cannot get up!"* I said I will be right there, I only work four miles from home. I got home and ran up the stairs to see Debbie lying in the bath tub with her head under the water faucet, I was so upset I grabbed her and lifted her out of the tub and walked her to the bedroom and helped her dry off and got her dressed. I helped her downstairs to the recliner, she said, *"I'm fine right her now, go head back to work and when you get home we might need to go back to the neurologist."* I asked, *"Are sure you are going to fine?"* She said, *"Yes, just give me the remote to the TV."* and she was going to watch her soaps.

No sooner than I got to work she called me and said, *"Dale I dropped the remote and tried to pick it up and fell out of the recliner and I cannot get up!"* I shot home and she called the doctor and he said, *"Get to my office as soon as possible."*

Once we got to his office, I had to hold her up while she was walking, He took one look at her and he said, *"Get her the hospital."* He said he still feels its MS but wanted to get her in to the hospital.

We drove to St. Joseph Mercy Hospital in Pontiac. We got a wheelchair and took her to the admitting counter and checked her in. Once we got her to the room she was starting to worry very much and I told her it's going to be alright. That evening I could see her ability to control her movements were becoming uncontrollable. She could not sit up without falling over. So Doctor Harding, Doctor Awsdi, neurologist, Doctor Rosenblack Infection Specialist, along with Doctor O'Hara, brain surgeon, they were all in her room trying to figure out what to do! I said please do something she is getting worse by the minute. Doctor Rosenbalack thought that she might had been affected by the Valley fever disease, since she was in Arizona for the winter and this was going around. The neurologist still stuck with MS. And Dr. O'Hara said we are not going to give her anything until we figure out what she has.

O'Hara wanted to perform a biopsy of one of the legions on her brain. He said it is a simple procedure, with the proper equipment. That was not going to be available until the 19th of August, three days from now.

Debbie was calm and we still felt it was MS, that's what we wanted to believe! The nurses were very nice and this hospital was really nice, Debbie had her own room so I could stay there. We called the kids and told them Debbie was going to have brain surgery on the 19th, I believe this is a Friday. Once we called Dylan and told him what was going on, he quit his job and was by our side within a few days. We told him not to do it but he refused to listen.

I remember I was helping here to the bathroom because by now she could not walk on her own. I was worrying very much but tried to hide it and I needed to be strong for her.

On the eighteenth the day before her surgery, she was having trouble with her hair and started crying and wanted a haircut. So I went to the front desk and asked the lady if the hospital had someone who cut hair that comes to the hospital. I explained to her Debbie's situation and she called her personal friend and she came to the hospital to Debbie's room and cut her hair. She was so happy and had the biggest smile on her face; I still to this day can see her happiness. That evening Debbie was nervous about the surgery she was to have in the morning. I reassured her that it was going to be fine and I was going to stay with her.

The next morning they wheeled her to the prepping room for the morning surgery, they shaved twelve spots on her head and placed these little targets in preparation for the MRI, these target points were to be feed into the GPS machine so this machine would drill the proper location and take a sample of the lesion that O'Hara wanted to test to confirm what she had. The Doctor said the surgery would only take about a few hours. So I kissed Debbie and I told her I will see her after the surgery, I told her that I love her very much and we are going to get through this and things will be fine. As they wheeled her down the hallway I saw a cross on the wall, I kiss my finger tip and touch Jesus, and said please help her.

I walked over to the surgery waiting area and had a cup of coffee and waited and waited for about six hours or so, until this receptionist came over to me and ask if I was Mr. Weatherford and I said yes I am. He said the surgeon wanted to speak to me in the consolation room. So I went in and sat down and waited for him to come in. Once he came in and sat down, he said Mr. Weatherford, I have the worst results I could give you, your wife has glioblastoma grade four. He said it is un-operate able because of the location of the tumor it was located in the front part of her brain in between the two-halves of her brain and was about 1 inch deep and about two inches diameter, the front part of her brain controls her motor skills that why it was affecting her movements . He said she may have six months at best! My heart fell to my feet! I could not believe this is happening to us. How do I explain this to her? I start crying like a little school girl, uncontrollable!

He said that he was sorry to give me this news but that was what she has, he said, *"We could start her on radiation and chemotherapy to help slow it down."*
I went out to the waiting room until Debbie was awake enough for me to see her. Once she came around she asked what the results were and I told her they were still working on it, I was unable to break the news to her just yet.

After she was able, they moved her to the fifth floor, this is the rehabilitation center, she was having trouble with the movement on her left side since the biopsy was performed on the right side of her head it affected the left side of her body movements. She had about thirty percent movement the left side of her body and her right side was still working well. I tried to let all of the nurses know that I did not want anyone to let Debbie know what she had, I was afraid she would give up the fight, I was not going to give up the fight. I wanted her to live, I could not picture me losing her. Dylan was going to fly out and stay with me and Debbie. Once Dylan arrived Debbie was so glad to see him, she said, *"I'm going to be fine you do not need to quit your job."* He said, *"No mom I want to stay with you and dad."*

By this time I went on family leave of absence from work to stay with Debbie as much as I could. I slept in her room and we would get up in the morning and I would feed her breakfast, oatmeal, two slices of toast and three milks.

Dr. Ezz was the radiation specialist and wanted to start radiation right away, and Dr. Farid was the chemotherapist, and wanted to start her on the chemotherapy capsules, as soon as possible as well.

The hospital allowed me to sleep in a fold out bed in her room. Because she needed help going to the restroom and she was having trouble pushing the call button if she needed a nurse, so I was there for her to help.

Dr. Ezz needed to fit her face with a mask for the Radiation so that Friday she was taken to the radiation clinic which was across the parking lot, so she had to go by ambulance because of the liability, so the paramedics had to come to her room and take her by stretcher to the ambulance to drive across the parking lot which was about two hundred yards away. Diluadid is her favorite drug of choice; she called it Kenny Rogers for the song "I just drop in to see what condition my condition was in." I remember when the nurses would ask her what her pain level was, she would always say it was an eight. I remember one night she turned to me and said, *"Dale can you score me some Diluadid."* This was so out of context for her to say but with the condition she was in I felt so sorry for her it was becoming so hard for me to bare. I was praying every minute of the day that God would let me kept her and not take her from me.

Her sense of humor never left her; she was so concerned about us and not herself. I remember her saying that when she gets cancer, she gives it to the entire family. By this time she seemed to be losing more and more of her motor skills I remember one day she started having seizers and as the day progressed they were getting worse and by evening the doctor said we need to get her in to intensive care unit so Dr. Harding and Dr. Amsaddii worked on Debbie until 1:00 am trying to get the seizers under control. By morning they moved her back to the seventh floor. Her left side is not working at all NOW and her right side is only about thirty percent, she no longer can get out of bed without me using this dolly to move her from the bed to the bathroom. Her vein can no longer be found so the doctor wanted to place a shunt in her chest, this would make it easier for the nurses to give her medication. Dylan was with us now so we would spend every moment with her. I slept next to her, I remember every morning around 4:00 am she would wake up crying so hard it was unbearable for me to hear and I would go to her side and comfort her! And tell her we are going to beat this Debbie. She wanted so bad to live and I could not bear the thought of losing her. So I would call the nurse, Jessie or Andrea. They would come in and give Debbie some medication to calm her down. At 6:00 am I would order her breakfast, oatmeal 2 slices of toast, and 3 milks and put the chemo capsules in her oatmeal. After this, we would talk and was so persistent that she took the capsules. I remember one morning, she was not taking the capsules like I wanted her to and I raised my voice at her and she said, *"Don't yell at me."* I just wanted her to get better and she wasn't. Once Dylan came in I would go home take a shower and come right back to the hospital. And start my evening all over again, the paramedics would come and pick up Debbie around 2:00pm to take her for radiation, and I would always try to have the nurses give her Diluadid before they took her and I remember one day they were picking her up and the paramedic asked if they gave her any drugs because he was complaining. He said it hard to move her when she was drugged, and I remember her saying, *"Suck it up big boy."*

After she came back from radiation she would be so drained for the rest of the day, but I was determined not to give up. One night there was a room full of friends and Debbie start to throw-up and she started choking and I could see in her face the panic because she could not move, so I turned her on to her side so she would not choke to death! After that she said I do not want to do the chemo capsules anymore they are making me to sick. I said that is fine but let's still do the rotation still. She agreed. By this time she was unable to move from the neck down. The head nurse on the seventh floor was concerned about her condition and we were thinking maybe we should try Henry Ford Hospital, so I asked for her the MRI discs, so Dylan took them to the Henry Ford Hospital for the brain cancer specialist to review them. They called me back a few days later and said we are sorry Mr. Weatherford but we cannot help her no more than what St Joseph Mercy hospital is doing for her. My heart fell to my feet once again. I remember one day when Joshua and Dylan was in her room and she asked if she should stop the chemo and I spoke up and said "yes" the boys would not answer her.

I spoke with the head nurse and she said that if Debbie got any worst she would not be able to leave the hospital, she is dying.

So Dylan and I started making plans to have her brought home. We had a hospital bed and all of the needed equipment sent to our house. I told Debbie we were going home and said "to Arizona" and I said no she started crying, *"I want to go to Arizona"* I said we can't but we are going home. So on September 21^{st,} we took Debbie home in ambulance and Debbie wanted for Joshua to come back to and see her so Joshua flew to our house and Big Debbie and Brenda her sisters were there along with Dylan and I. She was comfortable at home. But as soon as we got home she stopped the radiation, so we went from home health care to hospice in the same day. Each morning Dylan and I would sit in the spare bedroom mixing the medication for the entire day to keep Debbie as comfortable as possible. By this time Debbie stopped eating and drinking, she would not want anything at all. She knew her time was near. Joshua would play her guitar, she loved hearing him play, I bet his fingers were sore by the end of the day but he kept playing for her.

In between his playing I would put on a CD for her, she loved to listen to her music, I remember her asking me to play a CD called "Dale loves Debbie" I said what you know Dale loves Debbie, so start looking at this CD no clue what she was asking for until I saw a CD in the buffet written on a CD with a magic maker and the light can on this was a CD that Gary Laible give me to give to Debbie when we were in Niagara Falls in July when went there, the story was that every year Gary would make Karen a CD for her birthday and Karen said I should do the same for Debbie so before we left to go back home Gary gave me this CD to give to Debbie, she remembered that how sharp he mind still was. She said I like that CD, Dale. After that CD was done I played some George Harrison music, the song was, "If not for you" Debbie started crying and I ask her what was wrong and said "If not for." I started to cry. She said *"Dale I will wait for you, we will be together again, as we were in the past. You better not do anything stupid."* I knew what she meant; I could not live my life without her. I did not know if I could go on without her.

Joshua needed to go home to Heidi and my grandson Miles, Heidi was pregnant with our second grandson, Isaac. I remember Debbie saying that she would never see her new grandson and that hurt us both so much. I remember her saying to me Dale you need to buy Joshua a banjo and told her I would and she also told Dylan that he needed to write our story. I thought that would be pretty hard since he was not with us in the beginning, so I knew that this was a task that only I could fulfill for "My Debbie"

She was strong, never complained one bit about herself, always concerned about us. I remember when I would be walking down the hallway and I would go into Debbie's room, I would say to her I'm here and she would say, *"I know I could hear your walk, I know the sound of your walk."*

I remember saying to the hospice nurse that between 4:00 am and 6:00 am I was not giving Debbie any more medication, she would start crying, Debbie no longer wanted to wake up and by this time I was praying to God to please take her, the nurse said go head and give her Diluadid between those times it will help calm her down.

So on September 26th, early in the morning Debbie was having trouble breathing. I called Karen, the hospice nurse, and she came over right away. She looked at Debbie and said I believe Debbie will not make it through the day. She said start giving Debbie diluadid and the adavan to get her breathing under control. I sat there with Debbie knowing that this is the end at 11:20 am she stopped breathing and Karen said she is gone now Dale, and I started crying, and within a few minutes she started breathing again and Karen said wow she is a strong lady she does not want to leave, than she stopped breathing again and of course she started breathing again a minute or two after that so Karen called in another nurse to sit with us. And at 1:59 pm she stopped breathing and the sun came shining through the front living room window right on her face. I knew that was it. The nurse called Karen up and Karen told her to call her back in a few more minutes because she knew that Debbie was determined to stay with us. But that was it, 1:59 pm she went to heaven. This was the saddest day of my life; my Debbie was no longer with me. It was like my heart was ripped out of my body and replaced with only half of my heart back. I sat and held Debbie's hand until 4:30 pm when the corners came to take her away from me. And then I still did not want to give up her hand, I did not want too. My love and soul mate was taken away from me!

Debbie and I always wanted to be cremated; she did not want to be buried. And once I posted that Debbie had passed away, our nephew Terry got on a plane from Japan and flew out to our house, he and Debbie were very close. He came to support me and the rest of the family. I thought that instead of a memorial for her we would have a "Celebration of Life" for her. Judy and Marilyn, her very close friends, help me with everything to make this a celebration of life a memoir moment. It was a very great day, Oct 8th, 2011.

Dylan and Terry were busy making a picture disc so we could have a picture slide show on the TV. I put together music that meant a lot to the both of us. We decorated the front of the house, had food brought in and a couple of tents with tables and chairs. Also I gave a speech of celebration of life for Debbie and Judy read a portion from the book called the DASH, it was a wonderful event and a lot of people showed up.

It felt so nice, but very hard to accept the fact she was gone. I really was having a very hard time. At least my family and close friends were there to help me cope. Heidi had come with her mom and dad; they drove out from Wisconsin because Heidi was so close to having Isaac she was unable to fly. After the celebration of life, Dylan and I went to our house in Arizona to kind of get away for a while. I was thinking about putting our Arizona house up for sale. Once I walked in the front door and said there is no way I can sale this house. It had Debbie's touch and it made me feel sad thinking I was going to sell her home. It was extremely hard to sleep there. I guess it was too early, my grieving to be there even with Dylan with me. One evening Dylan and I was sitting in the back yard, leaning by the wall and he said to me, *"Dad I hate to say this, but I think it was the best thing that mom went before you, because I don't think she could of handed you going first, she would not deserve that pain for the rest of her life."* That was a bit of a relief to me but still hurt pretty bad. I was not ready for her to leave me, we had a lot of things we still wanted to do in life. Thinking back when she was at home in her last days I remember her saying, *"Dale you need to let me go."* I told her I could not let her go; until the last couple of days of her life, one evening I told her that she could go and I remember her saying *"thank you Dale."* That was the hardest thing I ever had to say and will be the hardest thing I will say during the rest of my life. I remember my favorite song to her while during our life together was a song by the Beatles was "In my life" this song was so true to my heart of how I felt all my life with her! And now the song that always stays in my head is a song by George Harrison "All things must pass." What a way to live out the rest of my life, not a good feeling at all. So while at the house in Arizona, I was going to spend a couple of weeks there, but it was so hard that I told Dylan I needed to go home, so we left the house early and went back to Michigan. Now I felt I needed to go to Ireland to take some of her ashes to her home land and spread some in her favorite places. So Dylan and I were on a mission, I thought that we should go on the Harp and Eagle that Debbie and I had been on several times in the past. We flew in to Dublin and took her ashes to every church we came across and I would sprinkle a little bit in the churches and I took some of her ashes to the cliff of Mohor and Galway Bay. And while we were there we visited Leap Castle and when we went there Sean Ryan the owner of the castle remembered me and asked where my wife was and told him she had passed. I told him that she always wanted to spend the night in his castle. He said, *"Dale you want to spend the night in my castle?"* I told him yes but could not do it on this trip, he said, *"Whenever you want to spend the night on my castle, just call me and I will arrange for you to stay."* This castle was his home and not for guests or open to the public for overnight stays. So after returning from Ireland I was thinking what a tribute to Debbie if I took both of the boys and spent a couple of nights in Debbie's honor with Joshua and Dylan.

So I made arrangements with the boys to go back to Ireland and once I told Jack Weaver what we were doing he said I would like to go with you and the boys too. I said that would be great, I would like that very much! I started thinking back when we went to Ireland in the past; Debbie would always look for local artist pottery and bring back home bowls or cups. I thought what a great idea if I took one of Debbie's pottery to Ireland to Sean Ryan to display in his castle. Debbie had made these three long stem cups, so I took one and wrapped it up and put it in my bag.

So on March 10, 2012 we flew to Ireland, me and the two boys and met up with Jack in Dublin. We spent a couple of days in there and took a train to Athone and I rented a car there and we drove to Leap Castle. Sean Ryan and his wife Ann greeted us with open arms, what a fabulous Castle. Sean cooked us a wonderful dinner I believe it was cabbage and ham. We sat around after dinner just listing to his stories and drinking Irish whiskey.

I told Sean that I brought him a piece of Debbie's pottery and asked if he would display it in his castle in honor of Debbie along with her picture and he said that he would be very pleased to do so. The sleeping arrangements were nice. Dylan slept on a blow up mattress, Josh slept on the couch and Jack and I slept in the wing that over looked the parlor on the second story of the castle.

We had such a wonderful time there. It was very kind of Sean and Ann to open their home to us. There kindness was overwhelming.

After two days at Leap Castle, we drove back to Athone and took the train back to Dublin, we stayed a couple of nights at the Clarence hotel, the owner of the hotel is Bono from U2 the rock band, along the Liffty River that was located in the Temple Bar area.

After returning home from Ireland I started getting involved with the American Cancer Society on Romeo Michigan. I decorated bags for the event and I was asked to give a speech that evening in honor of Debbie, and why the Cancer Society meant so much to me. So that evening when I was called to the stage I was able to walk right up to the microphone and I read a speech I prepared for this event.

"RELAY FOR LIFE"

"Hello everyone, I'm glad to see such a great turn out for this "relay for life" event. My name is Dale Weatherford and I would like to share with you all, why I feel the American Cancer Society "relay for life" is so important.

You really don't get the true concept of the "American Cancer society" until it affects you personally, or someone you love.

My wife lost her brother few years ago to melanoma cancer that affected his brain at the age of fifty-three. I remember my wife Debbie was feeling very helpless and sad. Thinking how this awful disease could affect our lives like this.

She actually decorated a bag for her brother and we both went to the relay for life event in Romeo Michigan, about two years ago, in honor of him.

On August 19th, 2011 my wife was diagnosis with geloblastoma brain cancer and five weeks later on September 26th I loss her to this awful disease. It came out of the blue with no warning. There was nothing anyone or anything could do to save her, I felt so helpless.

I watch my soul mate die before my eyes and there was nothing I could do to prevent this from happening.

You see I meet Debbie when she was 8 years old and I was 11. We were married at the age of 14 and 17 happily married for 38 years, 5 months, and 19 days; she just turned 53 years old when I lost her. I miss her every waking moment of my life."

After my speech that night that night I was feeling so proud that I was able to stand in front of a large group of people. I was leaving and had a few people come up to me as I was leaving and complimented me on a wonderful speech.

In July 2012, I was thinking about Debbie's fifty-fourth birthday up in August and I wanted to do something special for that day. I had been hanging out at this bar and grill called Oscar's down the street from my house and I had become very close with the manager, Sean and all of the girls there. I thought why not have a birthday party in honor of Debbie at Oscars? So I spoke with Sean and asked if I printed up Debbie shirts would he allow the staff to wear them on August 8th in honor of my Debbie and he said that would not be a problem. So I printed up about fifty shirts and I invited the ladies from Debbie's bowling team and her friends and we had a wonderful time, Sean even put up the neon sign outside saying "Happy Birthday Debbie Weatherford, Love Always Dale."

I decided to make another trip back to Arizona, this time it was not so bad. I felt very relaxed at our home this time. So I went hiking every morning, so I could talk to Debbie as I would be hiking, not sure if she could hear me but if so, she knew that she is always on my mind.

I grabbed her GPS and started going to the places she went last, like the casino and to Goldfield ghost town and as I was there I wrote what was on my mind about why I'm still here on earth, and what the reason I'm here is, why did God leave me behind.

I was at the" Gold Field" ghost town Arizona that was booming in the 1890's .I walk into this old little church there and sat down to say an prayed to the lord to keep Debbie safe until I could join her again.

I took a walk to this old town's cemetery that was tucked away on the   out   skirts   of   town. I was standing in a cemetery and I was trying to read the marker on the grave sites, most of them were unreadable. I was thinking how many people realized or past this way to this corner of this old town, to read these forgotten people's names in this little cemetery? Debbie did not need a marker or a grave site.

I'm her moving marker... to tell as many crowds of people "Debbie's Story." My words will spread faster than any marker in any cemetery could.

After a wonderful and peace fulltime in Arizona, I returned to Michigan, my dearest Heidi was doing a walk in honor of Debbie in Lacrosse Wisconsin. And of course I needed to be there with her and my son, Joshua along with my little grandson "Miles" a gift from God. Heidi's still carrying Isaac, she is due in November.

We all wore Debbie shirts I had printed up and it was a real nice thing to do for my Debbie, I had a lot of pleasure in doing this, and seeing my family.

After a couple of months went by I received an e-mail from my niece. Lisa had wanted to join a Relay for Life for the American Cancer Society in Centennial, Colorado. I was so happy that she was doing this for Debbie I sent her Debbie shirts for her mom and dad, Bobbie and

Jack. Later to find out that Jack and Bobbie had already scheduled a vacation for that weekend. Lisa was very disappointed that they would not be there to walk with her. So I thought about it for a while and came to the conclusion that I would not have her do this event by herself.

I called her up and told her that I will walk with her and she seemed to be very pleased with my decision. To join her for the event. Lisa and I walked from; I believe 5:00 pm until 3:00 am, stopping only to eat a hotdog. We figured out we walked twenty-six miles that night, we kept each other going by talking and sharing special moments with Debbie and her soul mate Chris. I felt so relaxed and peaceful, I feel we connected and now we have a lot in common to share. And actually I had been going to church every Sunday; my soul needed it, because when I die I will do anything to be with my Debbie, that's what I live for.

Since then I had gotten baptized at my church that made me feel a bit closer to God and Debbie. One day after church I felt I needed to go on another adventure with Debbie's ashes and I thought what better place to take some of her ashes then the Holy Land, Israel. So I did a bit of research and found this tour called American and Israel tour.

I booked the trip and took some of Debbie's ashes to spread in the most Holy places on earth. The western wall, Calvary hill, and old ruin where Christ did some of his ministry work.

I feel now my adventure with Debbie's ashes are complete, I still take my traveling Debbie everywhere I travel, either for work or pleasure, she is with me all the time. And when I die I know that I will be with her, because she said so, and she was always right!

Below are some of the e-mails that were sent to and from me on Debbie's condition during the hardest days of my life! Also below are all the emails, letters, pictures, and my speech to the American Cancer Society.

Speech for the "American Cancer Society" Eastern University of Michigan Conference

September 21st 2013

Hello all! My name is Dale Weatherford. I would like to express to you the reasons the American Cancer Society means so much to me. You see, four years ago I did not think much about this organization until my wife's brother died of melanoma brain cancer at the age of 53. My wife, Debbie, was so devastated by the loss of her brother that we decided to get involved in the American Cancer Society events. We did the relay of life in Romeo in 2009 in honor of her brother. Then, in 2011 on August 19th, my wife was diagnosed with gliablastoma brain cancer. The tumor was in the front of her brain which is the part of the brain that controls motor skills. She only survived 5 weeks after the diagnosis. On September 26, 2011 I watch my soul mate and lifelong friend die ..... In body, but not in soul. I felt so helpless because there was nothing I could do to save her. She was only 53. Debbie was not only my wife, but my friend. You see, we grew up together. I met Debbie when she was 9. I was 11 at the time. We were married at the age of 14 and 17 and were so much in love with each other. We were married for 38 years 5 months and 19 days. I will never forget our life together and our experiences. When Debbie was taken away from me, it felt like my heart was ripped from my body. I felt like an empty shell and still do to this day. This cancer has to be cured so no one will ever need to experience the pain that Debbie and I had to go through as well as our family. I miss Debbie with my every waking moment. I think of her when I go to bed and when I wake up and throughout day. She was truly an angel. Debbie was never concerned about herself, even when she was paralyzed from the neck down. She would say, "When I got cancer, I gave it to my family". I remember when the nurses would ask her if she was comfortable. She would look at me and ask, "Dale, do I look comfortable?" I would say, "Yes you do. Then she would say to the nurses, "I'm comfortable".

After Debbie's death my sons and I were at our house in Arizona sitting in the back yard. My son Dylan said to me, "Dad, I hate to say it, but it's a good thing that mom went before you. I don't think she could have handled the pain of losing you. You will need to endure this pain for the rest of your life, dad".

The last time I went to Arizona, I went to a ghost town that was booming in the 1890's called "GOLD FIELD". I went to the local church there and prayed to the Lord to keep my Debbie safe until I could join her. As I was walking around, I spotted a small cemetery that was tucked away on the outskirts of town. I went over to it and tried to read the names on the headstone markers on the grave sites. Most of them were unreadable after all the years. I thought of how many people passed this way to this corner of town to read these forgotten names. I knew that my Debbie did not need a marker or a grave site. I'm her marker and her epitaph. As I share the life of my Debbie and the wonderful person that she was, my words will spread faster than any marker in any cemetery ever could.

Your support of the American Cancer Society can help find a cure for the awful thing we know as cancer. It is my hope that no one else has to lose their soul mate because of this ghastly disease. Thank you!

Sent: Tue Aug 16 19:14:51 2011
Subject: DEBBIE!

Jeff / Tim

Debbie is back in the hospital, I'm here with her now. We went to see the neurologist this evening and he notice that she is getting worst, her whole left side is getting very weak as you know from the falls she had today.
He is afraid that she has a brain infection or a fungus on the brain, either way he said they cannot wait any longer because of the damages that is being done. They will be doing the bio. Of the lesions on the brain in the morning.

Sent: Aug 16, 2011 9:07 PM

Hello Jim,
Debbie is back in the hospital, I'm here with her now.
We went to see the neurologist and he notice that she is
getting worst and she also fell twice today, her whole
left side is getting very weak.
He is afraid that she has a brain infection or a fungus
on the brain, either way he said they cannot wait any
longer because of the damages that is being done. They
will be doing the bio. Of the lesion on the brain in the
morning.
I just want you to help me pray I need all the help I
can get!

Dale,

I don't want to overstep my bounds, but if you would
like Lisa and I to come and pray with you and Debbie at
the hospital, just let us know and we'll be on our way.
We completely understand if you would rather have your
privacy too. We have prayed together tonight and will
continue to. Lisa is going to circulate it through our
prayer-chain at our church tomorrow morning as well.
Try to get some rest.
Jim Hudson
I Chronicles 16:11

From: Dale Weatherford [mailto:dalew@odysseytooling.com]
Sent: Thursday, August 18, 2011 6:30 PM

Subject: Re: Deb

Well,
We had a long night and day,
Yesterday we were trying to have the surgery done, the neuro surgeon
the infectious diseases and the neurologist all (3) of these doctors were
here and they were trying to determine what direction to go in and what
disease to treat, none of the results. They been getting gave them any
clue so they were trying to set up the surgery room last night but they
were un able to schedule it, the equipment needed was unavailable. The
machine is called
Neuro navigation unit, that will do the actual surgery by using the MRI
information feed to the computer this well actually locate the spot that is

programmed to biopsy. So it is scheduled for 7:30am tomorrow
I'm doing everything to keep here comfortable,
The surgeon said it should take about 2 hours to perform the surgery, the
thing we need to look out for is bleeding if they cut a blood vessel, and
have trouble with bleeding, but I don't even want to think about that.
I will keep you posted

Thanks for the update. I prayed this morning. Lisa is
too. She's been asking for updates. I'll let her know.
Praying for you too Dale!

Dale,

I heard about your wife's illness last week and my families
thoughts and prayers are with you and your family. No matter how
crazy the world or our day to day jobs get, it is family that makes it
all worthwhile. Take care of your wife first and we will cover your
work end of things until you get back.

Keep in touch and let the team know if you need anything.
| **Mark Media**

 From: Mr. Dale Weatherford
To: 'jimhudson@att.blackberry.net'
Subject: Debbie
Sent: Aug 24, 2011 8:41 AM

I feel it will be very nice if you and your wife will
visit Debbie here at the hospital room 435 St Joseph
Mercy Okland , in Pontiac

Dale,

Would it be ok to ask what the prognosis is? I know she
had the biopsy on Friday but haven't heard anything
direct since then. I heard some "grapevine ramblings"
but I don't want to assume anything.

Jim Hudson

From: Dale Weatherford <dalew@odysseytooling.com>
Date: Wed, 24 Aug 2011 07:42:24
To:
'jimhudson@att.blackberry.net'<jimhudson@att.blackberry.
net>
Subject: Re: Debbie

Jim,
Glioblastoma Brain cancer,

Dale,

I am more sorry than I can say. Lisa and I can be there
around 6:30. This evening. Is that an ok time?

Jim Hudson
I Chronicles 16:11

Hi Dale,
Still praying for you and Debbie like crazy. It was
nice to visit with you both.
I messed up my ankle on my mountain bike so I've been
out of commission for a few days. Actually, I'm on my
way home from the docs right now.

The reason I'm writing is: a couple of ladies at my
church who have been praying for Debbie, fervently would
like to come visit her so they can put a face with the
prayer and just get to know her. They asked me to ask
you if it's ok. They know that this makes some people
uncomfortable and that is why they are asking if it's
ok. They would just like to meet her and encourage her.
If you'd rather them not, just say so. I've advised
them on her not knowing everything and they have to be
very careful what they say.

So just let me know your thoughts on that. Lisa could
probably come with them if that helps.

Take care Dale. Praying for you both everyday.

Jim Hudson
I Chronicles 16:11

From: Dale Weatherford <dalew@odysseytooling.com>
Date: Mon, 29 Aug 2011 14:15:40
To:
'jimhudson@att.blackberry.net'<jimhudson@att.blackberry.
net>
Subject: Re: Debbie

Jim,
Thank you for your prayers, at the moment we are
experiencing another set back she started having secures
today the body shivers out of control and stops and
starts again this lasted for hours before the new meds
kick in. Right now they are having a Cat scan done to
see what is going on, they might move her from rehab
back to neuro science floor, the medication seam not be
working as good as before, she has lost control of her
bladder as well, I will let you know when she is stable
and ready for visitors but I do not think now is a good
time.

Thanks for letting me know Dale. We'll keep praying.

Jim Hudson
I Chronicles 16:11

 From: Dale Weatherford
Sent: Sunday, August 28, 2011 10:29 PM
To: Jeff Golombeski
Subject: Re: IMG00058-20110821-1054.jpg

I just got home, she is still in the hospital she is in
rehab trying to learn to walk, her left side in not

talking to her to the brain and she is not taking it
well.

From: Jeff Golombeski
To: Dale Weatherford
Sent: Sun Aug 28 22:03:18 2011
Subject: RE: IMG00058-20110821-1054.jpg

Will she be able to walk with re-hab? When does she come
home? Are you going to take some time off?

From: Dale Weatherford
Sent: Monday, August 29, 2011 7:31 AM
To: Jeff Golombeski
Subject: Re: IMG00058-20110821-1054.jpg

We are not sure if she will walk again, she is still in
rehab, and wants to go home she is very upset, you know
how hospitals can be. I'm planning on coming back to
work next week my son Dylan -god bless his sole, will be
here this thursday to help me take care of her so I am
able to return to work,we start radiation this friday
and kemo next tuesday.

From: Jeff Golombeski
To: Dale Weatherford
Sent: Mon Aug 29 07:33:29 2011
Subject: RE: IMG00058-20110821-1054.jpg

Dale my very good friend,I have chills as I read this,it
must be cancerous from the treatment she will have.I
will do anything possible to help you with what ever you
need.Please let me know of anything you need. GOD BLESS
THE WEATHERFORDS'

Regards
| Jeff Golombeski

From: Dale Weatherford
Sent: Monday, August 29, 2011 10:57 AM
To: Jeff Golombeski
Subject: Re: IMG00058-20110821-1054.jpg

Thank you Jeff, I plan on returning to work next week.
My son Dylan is coming home this week, he went back to
California to pack all of his belongings coming back to
Michigan and leaving a real good job to help me with
Debbie.
She does not seam to be getting better as much as we
expected her too.
The doctor has her on anti- secure medication, it
starting not to work very well anymore. Her body shivers
like she freezing cold, and then it stops, that's
starting to worry me even more.
With dylan here that will help a lot, he is a blessed
son, could not ask for any better support.
The nurses here are fantastic and very understanding, we
are to meet with the rehab doctor today at 2:30 and he
will let us know when he feels she can go home. But my
problem is that we live in a by- level house when you
enter the house you either 7 steps up or 7 steps down.
Dr Farid came in and was saying they might send her home
this friday,I'm not sure if that a wise ideal.
She also lost control of her bladder.
What a mess things are in.

Keep faith and bless your son for the support!I wil be
home tomorrow and look forward to seeing you when we
have time.

Regards

| Jeff Golombeski

From: Dale Weatherford

To: Steve Foster; Keith Casebolt
Sent: Tue Aug 30 04:57:24 2011
Subject: DEBBIE

Update,
Last night was a set back she started having
uncontrollable secures,that started early morning and
into the night, they got more intense as the day went
on.
Nothing they gave her stop them.
They did a CT scan and seen bleeding from the biopsy in
an area of the brain this was causing pressure on the
tumor that was triggering the secures.
They move her back to ICU for monitoring her condition.
They started her on dalotted or something like that it
the drug that is 10x stronger than morphine. Around
11:30pm last night the secures stop, with a mixture of
drugs. Her Dr. Harding and her Neurologist Addmsaddi
were here till after midnight work to get her stable.
This morning Dr. "O" Hara the neuro surgeon that
performed the surgery will be here soon to review what
going on with the bleeding.

Dale,
I sure hope they can do something for Debbie today.
If there is anything I can do please make sure you call
me and I will be right there for you.

Ginger and I are thinking of you and Debbie. Talk to you
soon buddy,

Regards

| Tim Scott

Dale,

Can I forward this email to our prayer chain at church
to get more people praying?

From: Dale Weatherford
To: Steve Foster; Keith Casebolt
Sent: Wed Aug 31 12:19:09 2011
Subject: DEBBIE

Update,
I seen the her Doctor Harding this morning to get a real
good feel of what she thinks about Debbie's condition.
 Dr. Harding had said "her condition are looking real
grim at the moment."
Her condition is not improving with the steroids. Dr.
Harding said "they will start the radiation and kemo
friday it would be a miracle if the radiation works",
the doctors want to keep her in the hospital during the
first treatments to see how she reacts to the treatment.
Harding said " the treatment my worst in her condition,
but if it does.... it will be up to me to stop the
treatments, and if I do stop the treatments she will
only last for a few weeks at the most."
So we will see come friday, if we see a MIRCLE!
I'm having a hard time being strong today.
I feel so sad!!!!!!
The hospital staff has been letting me sleep here with
her during the nights, and she is in a private room
that's real nice of them.

Yes, 743 she does not know that her time here is short,
if she did she would give up and I cannot let that
happen, you understand.

----- Original Message -----
From: Jeff Golombeski
To: Dale Weatherford
Sent: Wed Aug 31 14:59:53 2011
Subject: Re: DEBBIE

Can I stop by tomorrow morning to visit? What room is she in?

From: Dale Weatherford
Sent: Friday, September 02, 2011 7:11 AM
To: Mark Media
Subject: Re: How's things

Hello Mark
Yesterday, she was fitted with her radiation mask, Dr Ezz said that the radiation treatment can not wait until tuesday, the cancer tumors are spreading to the right side of the brain so he wants radiation to start tomorrow morning.
Dr Farid the oncology will start the kemo tomorrow as well.
Hope this all works out, please help me pray for her that this all works out, I 'm not going to give her up to this disease, I will fight to the bitter end.

Dale,
My prayers are with you my friend. Fight the fight and stay as positive as you can at beating this monsters ass. It will be difficult and it will be trying, but the love of a good woman is worth all of that and more.

| **Mark Media**

From: Dale Weatherford
To: Steve Foster; Keith Casebolt
Sent: Fri Sep 02 18:18:38 2011
Subject: DEBBIE

Update,
Radiation and chemotherapy was started today, Debbie has been out complete ever since 9:00am after they gave her meds this morning, unable to communicate to her or get a

response out of her, she like in a deep sleep . We will
see how tomorrow looks.
They will continue the chemotherapy (pill form)
everyday for 2 weeks but the radiation will not start
back up until tuesday, the office is closed until then.

From: Dale Weatherford
To: Steve Foster; Keith Casebolt
Sent: Sat Sep 03 20:27:55 2011
Subject: DEBBIE

Update
This morning she was still out of it, radiation and
chemotherapy wore her out friday. She came around about
11:00 am this morning. She is a lot weaker, starting to
losing moment in her right leg and arm, and her neck,
can not control her head from moving side to side.

Not sure if its from the radiation or the chemotherapy,
or the cancer, I can not get a straight answer from
these doctors on the out come, they keep saying we are
in a holding period to see what the treatments will do,
they say it all depends on her system if or if not the
treatments will help. .
No radiation treatments until tuesday. The chemo will
continue through the weekend.
I was able to talk to her some today and carry on some
what of conversations until the strong meds kick in,
again.
 I'm still saying to her that she is coming home, and
I've will continue to believe that, I will not give up
hope. I have faith in gods healing powers.
Dylan made it in last night so he is here to help me
with her, I glad he is here I do not think I could
handle this alone.
I'm still sleeping at the hospital every night, its hard
for me to leave her alone at night, if she need help at
night I'm here when she calls my name, I honestly do
not believe she can't even push the call button for the
nurses if she needs something at night.

From: Dale Weatherford
To: Steve Foster; Keith Casebolt
Sent: Sat Sep 03 20:27:55 2011
Subject: DEBBIE

Update
This morning she was still out of it, radiation and
chemotherapy wore her out friday. She came around about
11:00 am this morning. She is a lot weaker, starting to
losing moment in her right leg and arm, and her neck,
can not control her head from moving side to side.

Not sure if its from the radiation or the chemotherapy,
or the cancer, I can not get a straight answer from
these doctors on the out come, they keep saying we are
in a holding period to see what the treatments will do,
they say it all depends on her system if or if not the
treatments will help. .
No radiation treatments until tuesday. The chemo will
continue through the weekend.
I was able to talk to her some today and carry on some
what of conversations until the strong meds kick in,
again.
 I'm still saying to her that she is coming home, and
I've will continue to believe that, I will not give up
hope. I have faith in gods healing powers.
Dylan made it in last night so he is here to help me
with her, I glad he is here I do not think I could
handle this alone.
I'm still sleeping at the hospital every night, its hard
for me to leave her alone at night, if she need help at
night I'm here when she calls my name, I honestly do
not believe she can't even push the call button for the
nurses if she needs something at night.

From: Dale Weatherford
To: Steve Foster; Keith Casebolt
Sent: Fri Sep 02 18:18:38 2011
Subject: DEBBIE

Update,

Radiation and chemotherapy was started today, Debbie has been out complete ever since 9:00am after they gave her meds this morning, unable to communicate to her or get a response out of her, she like in a deep sleep . We will see how tomorrow looks.
They will continue the chemotherapy (pill form) everyday for 2 weeks but the radiation will not start back up until tuesday, the office is closed until then.

From: Dale Weatherford
To: Mark Media
Sent: Fri Sep 02 05:10:47 2011
Subject: Re: How's things

Hello Mark
Yesterday, she was fitted with her radiation mask, Dr Ezz said that the radiation treatment can not wait until tuesday, the cancer tumors are spreading to the right side of the brain so he wants radiation to start tomorrow morning.
Dr Farid the oncology will start the kemo tomorrow as well.
Hope this all works out, please help me pray for her that this all works out, I 'm not going to give her up to this disease, I will fight to the bitter end.

From: Dale Weatherford
To: Steve Foster; Keith Casebolt
Sent: Mon Aug 29 09:37:58 2011
Subject: DEBBIE

Steve,
A short update,
 I plan on returning to work next week, GOD welling.

My son Dylan is coming home this week, he went back to California to pack all of his belongings coming back to Michigan. He is giving up a real good job to help me with Debbie.

She does not seem to be improving as much as we
expected her too. The brain is not communicating with
the left arm and leg as it should, walking is out of the
equation right now.
The doctor has her on anti- secure medication, insulin
and some other medications.
 The medication for anti secure is not working very well
anymore. Her body shivers like she freezing cold, and
then it stops, that's starting to worry me even more.
 They also have he on insulin for diabetic, but she is
not diabetic I think its from all of the steroids they
are giving her, and some other medication that is 10x
stronger then morphine for the pain she is having.
With Dylan returning home that will help a lot, he is a
blessed son, could not ask for any better support.
The nurses here are fantastic and very understanding
they let me sleep here at night so I can be by her side.
She always letting me know "the brain has not left the
station yet" she still has a sense of humor.
 We are to meet with the rehab doctor today at 2:30 and
he will let us know when he feels she can go home. But
my problem is that we live in a by- level house when you
enter the house you either 7 steps up or 7 steps down.
I'm looking into have a lift install along the stair way
so I can move her from upstairs to down stairs.

Dr. Fared came in and was saying they might send her
home this Friday. I'm not sure if that a wise ideal, in
the current condition.
She also lost control of her bladder, which started,
this morning, another obstacle for us to deal with...
What a mess things are in, but I'm being very strong no
more tears, we just need to drive forward, and do
whatever I can to make her comfortable, I know that GOD
bless me, for having her all these years.
Thank you for your support and understanding in my time
of need.

From: Dale Weatherford
To: Jeff Golombeski; Tim Scott
Sent: Sat Sep 03 20:26:46 2011
Subject: Re: DEBBIE

Update
This morning she was still out of it, radiation and
chemotherapy wore her out Friday. She came around about
11:00 am this morning. She is a lot weaker, starting to
losing moment in her right leg and arm, and her neck,
cannot control her head from moving side to side.

Not sure if its from the radiation or the chemotherapy,
or the cancer, I cannot get a straight answer from these
doctors on the outcome, they keep saying we are in a
holding period to see what the treatments will do, they
say it all depends on her system if or if not the
treatments will help. .
No radiation treatments until Tuesday. The chemo will
continue through the weekend.
I was able to talk to her some today and carry on
somewhat of conversations until the strong meds kick in,
again.
 I'm still saying to her that she is coming home, and
I've will continue to believe that, I will not give up
hope. I have faith in gods healing powers.
Dylan made it in last night so he is here to help me
with her, I glad he is here I do not think I could
handle this alone.
I'm still sleeping at the hospital every night, its hard
for me to leave her alone at night, if she need help at
night I'm here when she calls my name, I honestly do
not believe she can't even push the call button for the
nurses if she needs something at night.

Diluadid is the drug of choose.

We are coming home tomorrow and I will be at work
Wednesday. I will stop in and see you both later this
week. Thank you for the update.

----- Original Message -----
From: Dale Weatherford
To: Jeff Golombeski
Sent: Mon Sep 05 16:13:19 2011
Subject: Re: DEBBIE

She has been a bit sick today being on the chemotherapy medication.
They also started her back on the steroids again and I do believe that is also helping her more.
Keith Casebolt and his wife Jodie stop in yesterday that was nice of him.
Tomorrow, will be a busy day for her with the radiation and the chemotherapy and most likely a lot of doctors coming in and out since today was a holiday.

I ran into Shawn Bellestri at this hospital, apparently his grandfather had a stroke and is in the hospital here.

From: Dale Weatherford
To: Steve Foster; Keith Casebolt
Sent: Fri Sep 09 18:51:46 2011
Subject: DEBBIE

Today was one of the hardest days so far, This morning Debbie started having secures again they had to call in the rapped response team to get the secures under control, her room was full of nurses and doctors, once that was done and under control.
The supervisor for the neuro surgery floor, Tammy stop me in the hallway and said that they was going to most likely release Debbie from the hospital and send her home, they feel they cannot help her anymore, and it would be best place for her to expired at home.

She said they were going to evaluate her condition and
if there is no improvement they are going to release
her.
This is not what I wanted to here right now.
After I went home to take a shower and had time to think
about what she said, I thought this was not fair to
Debbie she has had only 5 of the 30 radiation
treatments. That not enough to judge progress.
I ran into to Tammy in the lobby of the hospital. I told
her if there is a glimmer of hope that she can improve I
owe her that much to her, I wanted her to stay in the
hospital and continue treatments and we will see if she
improves. I will work with her more to try to regain
control of her left arm and leg as well as her neck, she
can not hold her head up by herself.
This evening she started vomiting and she was choking on
her own vomit. We had to flip her over so she could
breed.
I contact the Henry Ford Hospital and there are clinical
trials for patients with glioblastoma cancer.
I'm getting a copy of her last MRI with contrast and my
son is going to run it over to the Neurological Surgery,
Steven Kalkanis office and they will review it and if
they can do something for her we will transfer her over
to the Henry Ford Hospital in west Bloomfield MI.

Dale,
Cancer is an ugly animal. It does things that make most of us just
scratch our heads and wonder why and/or how. Take care of her
the best that you can and keep the family as close as you can. And
should you have to make that tough decision to bring her home, do
so knowing that it is probably the way that she would prefer things;
don't make a fuss but keep the family close by your side.

Good luck my friend and we will keep you, your wife, and your
family in our prayers.

| Mark Media

From: Dale Weatherford
To: Jeff Golombeski
Sent: Wed Sep 14 17:34:20 2011
Subject: Re: Debbie

She is about the same as yesterday, except she actually raise here right are and open and close her fist, that happen a couple of times but that was exciting to me! Hope she gains more movement.

Tomorrow I should here from Henry Ford Hospital. Still staying positive!

From: Dale Weatherford
Sent: Saturday, September 17, 2011 7:39 AM
To: Jeff Golombeski
Subject: Re: Debbie

Hello Jeff,
Not to bad this morning, no radiation for Debbie on the week ends so that good. Receive a call back from Henry Ford Hospital yesterday and their is nothing they can do other than what is being done here for her, So I'm in the process of getting her home next week. We will still do the radiation and chemotherapy for the duration required and see where that takes us, I still will help her fight this cancer.
From: Dale Weatherford
Sent: Sunday, September 18, 2011 6:21 PM
To: Mark Media
Subject: Re: Sunday

Hello Mark,
I appreciate your kind words.
I know it comes from the heart.

My wife seems to be fading from me and I see the twinkle in her eyes disappearing. it's creating a void in my heart and soul that hurts so bad..

We will be taking her home from the hospital this coming week.
Not much more can be done here.

She surly is a fighter I don't know how she does it, but it is wearing her out.
I think she is getting ready to give up this fight.
I'm not sure if she is wanting to continue radiation and chemotherapy anymore, it's taking a lot out of her.
I'm going to leave that up to her to make that choice.

My other son will be here on tuesday and so will her big sister Deborah.

Dale,

Sorry to hear that things are not so good. Her fighting ability must mean that she wants to be home where things matter. I lived thru this with both of my parents, and being home when things were getting near the end is what they wanted more than anything. Hospitals are a place of many great things, but home is where it seems that things start and they should end; with as much family around as possible.

The void that you are feeling in your heart is pure and simple, the love of a good woman; so very hard to capture but so wonderful when it happens. I think to myself how lucky I am to be with my wife. Cherish the days that you have with her and the history that the two of you share will never end.

Good luck and God bless you and your dear wife.

| Mark Media

From: Dale Weatherford
To: Keith Casebolt; Steve Foster; Jeff Golombeski; Tim Scott
Sent: Wed Sep 21 20:16:15 2011

Subject: DEBBIE

Update,

Thank you Odyssey for the very nice fruit arrangement, I was able to get Debbie to eat a strawberry tonight that was a lot of work.

Today, they brought Debbie home by ambulance.
I had a hospital bed delivered and sat it up in the living room.
She stop taking the chemotherapy capsules they make her sick, she stop those a couple of days ago. She does not want to do radiation anymore, she stop that yesterday, I ask why she said, " would you like to go on living like this, unable to move your body?"
What could I say.... I could not argue with that statement.
She said, she is ready to die, she can accept that now, and she wants to go now.
I was shown how to give her all of the needed medications by the nurses, to prevent the seizures, as well as the pain and the anti- anxiety meds.

(She takes a lot of medication.)
Her body seems to be shutting down, she eating very little and is not hungry does want to drink anything, and she is sleeping a lot, I think she is closing up inside does not want to talk much, keeps her eyes close a lot.

From: Mr. Dale Weatherford
To: 'jimhudson@att.blackberry.net'
Subject: Re: Hello
Sent: Sep 22, 2011 12:16 PM

Hello Jim,
We brought Debbie home yesterday. She is no longer doing chemotherapy or radiation. She has basically given up

and is ready to see god and go to a better place.
Hospice is helping me.

Hi Dale,

I just wanted to say "hello" and let you know that we
are still praying for you, Debbie and your family.

Jim Hudson
I Chronicles 16:11

From: Mr. Dale Weatherford
To: 'jimhudson@att.blackberry.net'
Subject: DEBBIE
Sent: Sep 24, 2011 11:00 AM

Jim,
Please have your church, if you would please, say a
prayer to GOD to release her from this human body and
take her to HEAVEN, she has suffered enough.

PLEASE!

O.k. Dale. I will honor your wishes.
I will contact the prayer team.

From: Dale Weatherford
To: Jeff Golombeski
Sent: Sun Sep 25 12:10:31 2011
Subject: Re: DEBBIE

Jeff,

That will be fine if you want to stop by my house. We are making Debbie as comfortable as possible, with the medications making sure she is heavily sedated. That what hospice said to do, now and wait.

Debbie Ann Weatherford
August 8, 1958 - September 26, 2011
I would like to take a moment of your time to thank each and everyone for there kind thoughts a prayers during the most unexpected and painful time in my life.

Your prayers and thoughts were felt by both of us, but god had other plans for my soul mate.
I would like to share a bit of my thoughts; she pass away at home with the family. She was not in pain, she was so beautiful and peaceful looking, when she pass.
Thank you all for your donations, which I used for the "Celebration of Life "on Oct, 8 2011.
I'm sorry that some of you were unable to attend for various reasons, I do understand.

Thank you and God Bless you all
Dale

I would like to raise a toast to MY lovely "Debbie" and until we meet again may god hold you in the palm of his hand.

Today is not a day of sorrow; it's a day of "celebration of life" for our Debbie.... She left us 12 days ago. Or 288 hours ago, it feels like it's been much longer.... as time seams to drag on for me.

I feel more bless today then ever before.... each and
every day since she has been gone.

I believe it's our love and companionship that we
shared together that I will miss most of all.... her
absent in my life now. I will always, need her by my
side and I know she would say... "Ditto."

I realize now what a major impact she has made to her
surroundings.
She has touched the souls many   more people then she
could ever have realized....

Her smile and the beautiful glow that radiated from
her soul have touched us all....
I still can and will always picture those beautiful
blue eyes that held that little twinkle I loved so
much.

I have spent most of my life here on earth with
Debbie, we were married 38 years, 5 months and 19
days before she pass away....

It's saddens me to think that I will never hear her
voice, or her laughter, or see her beautiful smile --
that always would light up a room....

Or see those blue eyes that always melted into my
soul... or smell her" moon light path" perfume. Or
ever hold her in my arms again...

That will be impossible for me to ever get use too...

I knew Debbie when she was only 8 years old. They
move away for about 5 years.

When we meet again in the early 70s there was this
special attraction, she had that caught my heart and
soul... it is hard to explain, but we knew that at
first sight, "it was true love,"

It was very hard in the beginning for us to set a
path in life that would be proper for us to start a
family...

We work hard to make the right decisions and our love

for each other grew stronger, we were so comfortable, with each other, there was never a doubt we were going to make it...

She was so strong, determine and independent women...

She was my rock and my soul keeper...

It hurts my soul now to live with this void that god has created....

During Debbie's illness,
I remember in her last days, she said that. "I would wait for you Dale."
That we were destined to meet in our next life, as we did before and as we will again and again...

She said that "I will stay by your side to keep you strong" in these times of need....and she would stay in my heart and soul until we are together again.....

My hope and dreams is that we together can help support, and fund this wonderful organization, in finding a cure to this awful disease. So no one will need to en dour the pain and surfing that my wife and I, as well as our family had to go through, as well as many other families in similar situations.

We need to continue to support and help this Society. I know I will in every way I can. Because of the pain this disease has created in my heart will never go away for me.

From: Dale Weatherford
Sent: Tuesday, October 25, 2011 4:25 PM
To: Jeff Golombeski
Subject: IMG00107-20111024-1604.jpg

Hello Jeff
I back at home, came in this morning on a red eye flight
arrived at 6:30 this morning.
Just need to get back it was very painful for me to stay
at our home in Az to long.
How are you and everybody doing,I might drop in around
the end of the week for a visit. I'm still leaving for
Ireland next week and after I return I will most likely
start back to work.
Here is a picture of debbie and a some of her ashes at
home in AZ the place she love the most.

Debbie at the age of 8 years old when I first laid eyes on her, can you see the glow in her eyes, " so beautiful."

Debbie 1966

Debbie at the age of 13, our hearts connected right away, if someone said" there is one such thing as love at first sight." I can say that they are most definitely wrong

Debbie and I as we were dating in 1972, we had not a care in the world, just that we loved each other and never wanted to be apart. We were so at ease with each other it was destined to be.

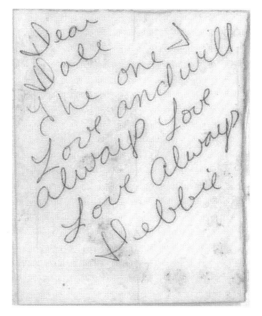

My birthday, what a" present" December 9th 1972

Debbie's 8th grade school photo, we were married shortly after this was taken. (She is wearing the same dress the day we got married)

Changing the year on our Birth certificates, we were too young to get married A girl needed to 16 with a parents signature, she was 14. A boy needed to be 18, and I was 17. This was the legal age in Las Vegas in 1973

The morning of April seventh 1973 Debbie was calling one of her friends' saying that she will no longer be going to school.

Jim Leonard, he played the role as her real father, we were off to Las Vegas!

Stopping on the way to Las Vegas for a bit to eat

The happiest day, we were "glowing" we were finally together for eternally

MAILING ADDRESS: P.O. BOX 26, ORANGEFIELD, TEXAS

BOOK 409   684979

Marriage Certificate

State of Nevada } ss.   No. A 458442
County of Clark. }

This is to Certify that the undersigned_____LEE SPEIRS_____
Did on the _7th_ day of _APRIL_   A. D. 19 _73_____
at_____LAS VEGAS_____Nevada
          (Address or Church)   (City)
join in lawful Wedlock___DALE LEE WEATHERFORD_____
of_____BELL_____State of _CALIFORNIA_____
and_____DEBRA ANN MORGAN_____
of_____WHITTIER_____State of _CALIFORNIA_____
with their mutual consent, in the presence of _JAMES LEONARD_____
and _GRACE WEATHERFORD_ who were witnesses.

Recorded at the Request of MARRIAGE COMMISSIONER
     Date   APR 17 1973   LORETTA BOWMAN, Commissioner of Civil Marriages
   in Book of Marriages, Clark County, Nevada.
   Records, Paul E. Horn, Recorder.
Fee $1.00 Indexed . . . . B. V. Deputy   (Sign this in official capacity.)

TO BE GIVEN TO THE RECORDER

Debbie and I living in Texas 1973

Enjoying life together

Debbie and I, with Alice, her mother

She loved animals, and we had our share

Enjoying our conversations together

Debbie loved the beach this were she belonged   (2009)

On the train going from Rome to Florence Italy, April 2011

Debbie last hair cut the night before her surgery 9/18/11

Oh my LOVE!!!!!!!!!!!

Debbie at home in San Tan Valley AZ. 10/2011

Debbie in Ireland 11/2011

Debbie in New Orleans 12/11/12

My Michigan friends I met in Ireland

Debbie innn Dublin, Ireland

Debbie in Enisse Ireland

Galilee Israel

Jerusalem Israel

Huntington Beach Ca.

Newport Beach Ca.

Lacrosse WI. At Joshua and Heidi's house (Miles Bed room)

Niagara Falls Canada

Seattle Washington

The Dead Sea Israel

Debbie picture in the western wall in Israel, the prayer I wrote on the back of her picture said " until we meet again my God hold you in the palm of his hands"

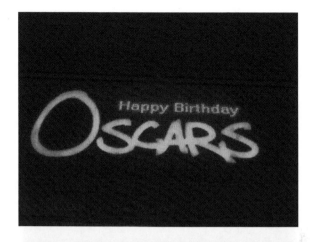

Debbie in Leap Castle, Ireland

Debbie's pottery and photo now on display in "Leap Castle"

Dylan, me, pookie ,Ann, Joshua, and of course Sean Ryan at Leap Castle

Debbie and Sean

Dylan, me and Joshua at Leap Castle enjoying our stay with Sean and Ann

Sean had kept Debbie's photo from the previous year next to this glass of water; he showed it to me and my sons when we came back the following year to spend a couple of nights at his castle.

Leap Castle

Lisa and I at "Relay for Life" in Colorado

Joshua, Isaac, Miles and Heidi

Jessica

Mark and Deborah (big Debbie)

Bobbie, Lisa and Jack

Marilyn, me and Judy

Reading my speech of relay for life Romeo MI 2012

Celebration of Life, Oct 8TH 2011

Terry my nephew, Josh, me and Dylan

Dylan, me, Frank and Joshua

You may be gone but you will live forever in my soul

Made in the USA
Charleston, SC
12 December 2013